BEOWULF

BEOWULF

In Blank Verse

translated by

RICHARD HAMER

FABER & FABER

First published in 2020
by Faber & Faber Ltd
Bloomsbury House
74–77 Great Russell Street
London WC1B 3DA

Typeset by Donald Sommerville
Printed in the UK by TJ International Ltd, Padstow, Cornwall

A CIP record for this book
is available from the British Library

ISBN 978–0–571–35215–9

FSC
www.fsc.org
MIX
Paper from
responsible sources
FSC® C013056

2 4 6 8 10 9 7 5 3 1

Contents

Introduction

Why does anyone need another translation of *Beowulf*? There are already numerous translations in existence, some currently in print, and others available online. They come in a variety of forms. Those in prose range from almost word-for-word versions, some of them pretty much unreadable and bordering on the incomprehensible, but perhaps of some help to those trying to master the language of the original, to others rather more modernised in their language and giving a readable account of the contents of the poem. Those in verse include versions aiming to reproduce as closely as possible the metre, alliteration and other characteristics of the original, others using rather looser forms, but still adopting some of the original characteristics, such as four-stress lines and a fair amount of alliteration, and a few in more formally structured verses, such as regular metres and even rhyme and stanzas. Anglo-Saxon poets had available a significant amount of special poetic diction, and translators use archaisms and the like to emulate this to varying extents.

Apart from the very close translations designed to help students and others to master the text, the intention of the translators is to convey to the reader with little or no knowledge of Anglo-Saxon the content of what is generally regarded as a highly skilful and important literary masterpiece from an early stage of the culture of the English nation. It may be that those who use some of the metrical and other tactics described above can achieve something of the desired effect for some readers, though in my own opinion and experience it is likely to be limited, and indeed in some cases an irritant.

Embarking on the translation, I decided therefore to do it in blank verse, since this has a certain but not excessive dignity and formality, which a poem of this sort needs, and to avoid almost entirely archaisms and poetic diction. The use of a freer form of verse seems to me to have no great merit; one might as well do it in prose.

The whole question of verse translations is discussed in detail by Hugh Magennis, *Translating Beowulf: Modern Versions in English Verse* (Cambridge, 2011), which I had not read when I started my translation, and which can be strongly commended to anyone interested in translation theory. Commenting on the only complete blank verse translation previously published, that of Mary E. Waterhouse, *Beowulf in Modern English: A Translation in Blank Verse* (Cambridge, 1949), he observes:

> Waterhouse has a certain logic on her side when she identifies blank verse as a kind of 'modern' (understood in its broadest sense) equivalent of Old English metre. But of course the adoption of blank verse brings a whole series of historical associations and connotations that profoundly alter the register and feel of the poem. Blank verse may be, or (more correctly) may have been, a kind of default mode of English verse but it is far from being a neutral medium. In Waterhouse's version we get a polished, classicized Beowulf.

He agrees with Edwin Morgan (translator, *Beowulf: A Verse Translation into Modern English*, Aldington, Kent, 1952, repr, Manchester, 2002), that 'Blank verse is no longer a living medium for extended writing,' and observes of Waterhouse's first three lines, which he quotes, 'This has dignity and formality, but it turns *Beowulf* into a "poetic" poem from the golden treasury of (post-medieval) English verse.' Noting her claim to be offering a clear and straightforward translation without archaisms, Morgan listed numerous such terms, giving the impression that the whole thing is full of them. There are in fact a fair number, but they are scattered about, and to my mind give nothing like the effect Morgan claims.

I had not actually been aware of the existence of this translation till I read about it in Magennis's book, and apart from the three lines he quotes I deliberately did not read it till I had finished my own. I was favourably impressed, though (being as dispassionate as possible) I consider that my own version, by virtue of a greater avoidance of archaism and a more fluent use of the verse form, reads rather better. I do not agree that blank verse carries with it 'historical associations and connotations', since it has been used in such various ways ever since its inception, and to my mind is as neutral as you can get.

I do not think it appropriate to offer an essay on the poem as a whole. With the reservations expressed above, I have tried to represent what the poet, or more precisely the manuscript, has given us as closely as possible, and anyone (and I hope there may be some) who becomes interested enough can easily follow it up among the many books and studies that have been published, including the introductions to the various editions and some of the other translations. There are places in the text where the sense is for one reason or another somewhat uncertain, but the issues involved are not of huge moment for the overall interpretation, so I have decided to offer brief notes only on the most significant of these.

The reservation expressed above about the poet may seem pedantic, but it has some point. *Beowulf* survives in only one manuscript, now in the British Library, written about the year 1000 and consisting of a compilation of prose and verse in Anglo-Saxon. It has suffered some damage over the centuries. We tend to think of the poem as it appears in the manuscript, begun by one scribe and completed by another, as the creation of one mind, allowing for the fact that these scribes made errors or copied already existing ones, some of which are obvious and others which may be undetectable, including omissions. Nothing is known about the identity of the poet, or even his rough date, though clearly he composed it before about 1000 when the manuscript was copied and, given the Christian allusions, unless we are to regard them as a later insertion, some time after the conversion, which began in 597. It is also possible that the 'original' poem may have been worked over to some extent by a later hand, but there is no way of knowing, and since as it stands the poem has a perfectly satisfactory general structure there is no point in speculating. However, the account below of some of the historical and legendary characters and events referred to may be of some help in understanding the more allusive passages and references.

As described above, I decided to use blank verse for my translation with the idea that this would make it more accessible to modern readers. The Old English language differed from modern both grammatically and syntactically in a number of ways, and so did the standard metre of their verse. (For those who would like to know, there are a number of websites which give a good succinct account of the Old English verse 'rules'; or see my own account on pp. xiii–xvii of *A Choice of Anglo-Saxon Verse*, revised and expanded edition, London, 2015). It has therefore been unavoidable that the translation should contain a fair amount of paraphrase.

THE POEM'S CONTENT AND BACKGROUND

The basic story is very simple. Hrothgar, king of the Danes, builds a great hall, probably at or near Lejre in Denmark, and names it Heorot or 'Hart'. Grendel, a monster living in wild country nearby, is enraged by the sounds of revelry, and attacks, slaying and eating many Danes. Beowulf, a Geat living in what is now southern Sweden, hears of this, and crosses the sea with a troop of his men, intending to defeat the monster. Grendel attacks his party in Heorot, but is mortally wounded. The Danes celebrate, but the following night Grendel's mother exacts revenge. Beowulf is led to her dwelling place in a hall beneath a mere, dives in and kills her, and, finding Grendel's corpse, beheads him and carries his head back to Heorot. He then returns home, laden with rewards, which he donates to the Geatish king Hygelac.

In time Beowulf becomes king of the Geats, and reigns successfully for many years. But a felon steals some treasure from a dragon's hoard, and the enraged dragon seeks revenge by burning the houses of those living nearby. The elderly Beowulf undertakes to tackle the dragon alone, but, when he has been seriously wounded, he is joined by a younger warrior, Wiglaf, and between them they slay the dragon; Beowulf, however, also dies, and is fittingly buried.

These fictitious events are set against a background of the wars, disputes and dynastic alliances of the various tribes in southern Scandinavia in the late fifth and early sixth centuries, the details of which can, with much uncertainty, be reconstructed from various historical references and their appearance in other literary works of the area which seem to be based on local memories. It is clear that the Beowulf poet could count on his audience knowing a fair amount about some of these characters and events. The broad facts are given here, partly in the following paragraphs, and partly in the notes at the end of the volume.

The various tribes and nations involved had a variety of appellations, and I have on the whole substituted the main one for the more unusual. The Shildings were the Danish royal family, and by extension sometimes simply the Danes; the Shilfings were the Swedish royals (it is unfortunate that these two names are so similar). The poet refers to the tribes in various ways largely in order to help his alliteration, so that there are apparently North Danes, East Danes, and even Spear Danes; but these are all in fact the same people. Likewise the Geats can be Weder Geats or just Weders. I have simplified all this.

Geographically the action takes place in southern Scandinavia, extending as far west as the mouth of the Rhine, where the historical Hygelac was indeed killed while on a raid in about 521, the only event in the poem that can be at all closely dated. Heorot is thought to have been at or near the modern village of Lejre in Denmark, not far from Roskilde. There are burial mounds in this area, and recent archaeological searches have found evidence of the early existence of substantial hall buildings. The name Roskilde seems to derive ultimately from *Hrothgar's kilde*, or 'Hrothgar's well'. The Geats appear to have controlled a substantial area of southern Sweden, with the Swedes themselves to the north of them. The fight at Finnsburg and its aftermath must have taken place somewhere within the Frisian area. Any more precise localisations would be difficult.

Except for Beowulf himself, all the characters mentioned below are presented as historical, and in most cases certainly were, as supported by other later accounts from northern Europe, mostly Norse, though one should bear in mind the vagaries of oral transmission, as a result of which some relationships, names and other details may well have become confused.

The main part of the Danish royal family appearing in the poem consisted of descendants of Shild, whose grandson Halfdane had three sons, Heorogar, Halga and Hrothgar, and a daughter, name unknown owing to a problem with the text, who apparently married the Swedish king Onela (see below). Hrothgar had two sons, Hrethric and Hrothmund, and a daughter, Freawaru, who in due course would be married to Ingeld, prince of the Heathobards, in the unsuccessful hope of settling a feud. Halga's son Hrothulf was an important figure at court, who joined with Hrothgar in defeating and slaying Ingeld after an attack which apparently included the burning down of the hall Heorot. On Hrothgar's death

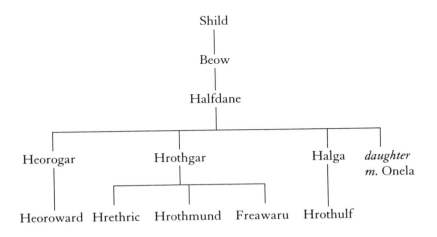

he usurped and deprived Hrethric of the throne. Heremod and Hnaf, the prince slain in the first phase of the Battle of Finnsburg (see below), were earlier members of the Danish royalty; Heremod went to the bad and is referred to as a contrast to the good kings.

Ongentheow, king of the Swedes, and a member of the family called Shilfings, had sons Ohthere and Onela; he was killed during a raid by Hygelac into his territory (the campaign is described in detail on pp. 124–7. It seems that Ohthere became king, and on his death Onela took power, causing Ohthere's sons Eanmund and Eadgils to take refuge at the Geatish court, and in an ensuing war Eanmund and Heardred the Geatish king were killed. Later, supported by the Geats, Eadgils attacked, and Onela was slain in turn, Eadgils becoming king. Since Onela had married the sister of Hrothgar, Beowulf's Geats were here fighting against the brother-in-law of his former patron.

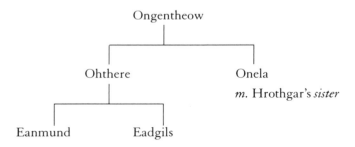

Hygelac, king of the Geats, was the son of Hrethel; his sister married Edgetheow, and they were the parents of Beowulf. Hygelac was killed during a raid on Frankish territory, and his son Heardred succeeded him, but was slain in a war with the Swedes, after which, as the poem has it, Beowulf became king.

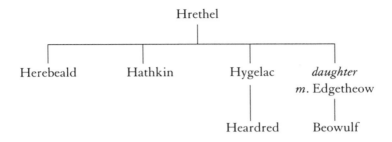

Hrethel
|
Herebeald Hathkin Hygelac *daughter*
              | *m*. Edgetheow
            Heardred Beowulf

The poem's account of the Battle of Finnsburg and its aftermath is given without including significant details, starting indeed after the main fight, showing that the audience was expected to know the story in some detail, as with the other historical events referred to above. A fragment of another Old English poem known as *The Fight at Finnsburg* gives further information, and a suggested reconstruction is given in the note to p. 46.

the note to p. 46.

PRONUNCIATION

I have on the whole given the names of the characters in a spelling intended to suggest to the reader the Anglo-Saxon pronunciation, in most cases merely modernising the spelling as necessary. The final *e* on some names (Romerike, Alfhere, Ashhere, Ohthere) needs to be pronounced, and the medial *h* in these should also be pronounced; the spelling *-ea-*, in many names including 'Geats', should be pronounced like the modern *-aie-* in *gaiety*. If the *y* in Hygelac's and Hygd's names is pronounced much like the vowel in modern 'huge', that will not be far wrong. I have cheated with characters whose names contain diphthongs, such as the *-eo-* in Beowulf, by using these sometimes as one and sometimes as two syllables to fit with the metre.

Beowulf in the manuscript is divided into 'fitts', an Old English word for 'divisions of a poem', indicated by the insertion of Roman numerals, and these are here retained, though sometimes they went slightly astray or were omitted, as briefly indicated in the Notes. In some cases they appear to divide a sentence, but they have been left as they were, except that omitted numbers have been supplied.

As one would expect, the manuscript, copied by two scribes, contains scribal errors, and it has also suffered a certain amount of damage of various sorts, so that some passages have had to be corrected or reconstructed; this has been convincingly done by various editors over the years, and details will be found in any of the more recent editions. There is, for example, an omission in fitt I which obscures the name of Hrothgar's sister, and there are a spate of problems in reading the text in the twenty or so lines covering the end of fitt XXXI and the beginning of fitt XXXII.

Endnotes are supplied on points which seemed to require explanation, and these are indicated in the text by symbols beside the lines concerned.

A feature of Anglo-Saxon verse which has been retained is the compound word, such as 'gold-hall' or 'shield-bearer', usually translating precisely the original. These were used partly to add variety and colour, and to facilitate the fairly strict alliterative pattern required by the 'rules' of their versification. For that reason I have also used alliteration as much as possible without distorting the sense to echo that practice, though without attempting to follow the patterns.

Overall I have kept as close to the manuscript as possible, and hope I have made no significant changes to its sense.

Acknowledgements

At university my tutor, Christopher Tolkien, inspired me to specialise in medieval literature, and I am glad to express my gratitude to him for that life-changing decision. He pointed me to Friedrich Klaeber's edition (*Beowulf and the Fight at Finnsburg*, 3rd edition, 1950), which remains the one I mostly use, and to which I feel enormously indebted. A thoroughly revised and updated fourth edition, edited by R. D. Fulk, Robert E. Bjork and John D. Niles, was published in 2008. For my translation, undertaken as a form of relaxation in old age, I am grateful to my former pupil and now friend Joe Winter, who has himself published a different sort of translation of *Beowulf*, as well as verse translations of the works of Rabindranath Tagore, Jibanananda Das and other Indian poets; he has kindly read drafts of my efforts and drawn my attention to infelicities; those that remain result from my obstinacy. My thanks are also due to Faber & Faber and in particular to Lavinia Singer and Matthew Hollis for their detailed care and guidance in the preparation of this book.

BEOWULF

*An account of Shild, founder of
the current Danish royal dynasty,
and his descendants and funeral.*

Hear! we have heard the stories of the might
Of kings of the Spear Danes in days gone by,
And how the princes practised valiant deeds.
 Often Shild Sheafing occupied the mead-halls
Of bands of enemies in many tribes
And made the nobles fear him, after first
He was found destitute. He lived to see
Comfort for this, he grew under the skies
And prospered honourably, till the time
That all the neighbouring tribes over the ocean
Had to obey him and to pay him tribute.
That was a good king. Later a young son
Was born to him within his royal courts,
Whom God sent as a comfort to the people.
He saw the dire distress that they had suffered
For a long time before, without a prince.
To him the Lord of Life, Ruler of Glory,
Granted success and honour in the world.
Beow was renowned, the fame spread far and wide
Of Shild's son throughout Scandinavia.
So must a youth by goodness bring to pass,
By generous gifts while in his father's care,
That later, in his age, when battle comes,

I

Good comrades will stand by him, folk be loyal.
By honourable deeds a man must thrive
And prosper everywhere among the tribes.
    Shild went his way at the appointed time,
In great age, to the keeping of the Lord.
His dear retainers bore him to the shore
As he himself, the ruler of the Shildings,
Commanded while he still had power of speech.
The much-loved leader long had ruled that land.
Down at the harbour stood the round-prowed ship,
Icy and ready to put out to sea,
The prince's vessel, and therein they laid
The treasure-giver, their belovèd lord,
Up on the ship, the great man by the mast.
There many precious goods from distant lands
Were piled beside him; I have never heard
Of any ship more fittingly supplied
With battle-gear and instruments of war,
With swords and corslets; in its bosom lay
A mass of treasures that would go with him,
Depart far off into the sea's domain.
They sent him with by no means fewer gifts
And treasures of the people, than did they
Who in the first place sent him forth alone
Over the salty sea-roads as a child.
They also raised a golden banner for him
High overhead; they gave him to the ocean,
Let the sea bear him off; their hearts were sad,
Their spirits mourning. Nobody on earth
Can tell for certain who received that cargo.

I

*Hrothgar becomes king and builds the
great hall Heorot, celebrations within
which provoke the monster Grendel.*

Then in the town was Beow of the Shildings
For many years the people's much-loved king,
Well known among the nations, when his father
Had parted from the earth, until to him
Was born great Halfdane; while he lived he ruled
The glorious Shildings, old and fierce in battle.
To him in turn four children altogether
Were born into the world, leaders of armies,
Heorogar, Hrothgar and the noble Halga.
The fourth, a daughter, as I heard became *
The queen of Onela, that well known king, †
The dear bed-fellow of the warlike Swede.
   Success in war was granted then to Hrothgar,
Honour in battle, and his noble kinsmen
Obeyed him readily, until the young
Warriors grew into a mighty band.
It came into his mind that he would order
A house, a mightier mead-hall to be built
Than any sons of men had ever heard of,
And there inside he would share out to all,
Both young and old, all that God granted him,
Apart from public land and human lives.
I heard that work was widely ordered there

From many tribes throughout this middle-earth
To decorate the dwelling, in and out,
And very soon that greatest banquet-hall
Was ready; he whose word was law throughout
The land of Denmark named it Heorot.
He did not break his vow, but shared out rings
And treasures at the feasts. The mead-hall towered,
High and horn-gabled; but in time to come
It would feel hostile fire and hateful flame;
Nor was it very long after that time *
That war between father- and son-in-law
Would break out, following a deadly feud.

    A mighty demon, one who dwelt in darkness,
Was moved to hostile anger when he heard
The sounds of merry-making every day
Loud in the hall. The music of the harp
Accompanied the clear song of the minstrel
Who, skilful in the telling of the story
Of mankind's origins in ancient times,
Recounted how the Almighty made the earth,
Glorious countrysides flowed round by water,
And set the brightness of the sun and moon
To give light for the dwellers in the world;
Next he adorned the regions of the earth
With leaves and branches, and created life
For every race of those that live and move.

    Thus the retainers lived a life of pleasures
In blessed manner, until one embarked
On violent crimes, a hellish enemy.
This angry spirit, Grendel was his name,
Haunted the moors and fens and fastnesses,
A powerful prowler of the border lands.

The hapless creature long inhabited
The land of monsters, after the Creator
Condemned him in the family of Cain.
The everlasting Lord avenged the crime
Of slaying Abel; angered by the feud,
He drove him far away from humankind.
From him all wicked progenies were born,
Ogres and elves and other evil spirits,
Likewise the giants who battled against God
For a long time; he paid them back for that.

II

Grendel repeatedly attacks Heorot.

Grendel set off to visit the great hall
After night came, to find out how the Danes
Had settled down after their beer-drinking.
He found therein a band of noblemen
Asleep after the feast; they knew not care,
The misery of men. The evil creature,
Greedy and grim, was ready straight away,
Savage and brutal, and seized thirty thanes *
From where they rested, then went out again,
Exulting in his booty, to go home
To his own dwelling with that fill of slaughter.
Then with the dawn, at the first break of day,
Was Grendel's violence revealed to men.
After the feast a wail of woe went up,
A loud cry in the morning. The great prince,
The noble chieftain, sat in grave distress,
Suffering grievous sorrow for his thanes,
When men had found the tracks left by their foe,
The cursed sprite. That struggle was too strong,
Fierce and persistent; for straight afterwards,
Just one night later, he again committed
More murders, for he suffered no remorse,
More feud and crime, on which he was intent.
Then it was easy to find men who sought
To take their rest in beds further away

Among the houses, when the unwanted guest's
Malice and violence were clear to see.
Those who had once escaped that enemy
Kept themselves further off and more secure.
And thus he ruled, fighting against the good,
One against all, and so that wondrous building
Stood idle. For a long while after that,
Twelve winters, did the ruler of the Shildings
Suffer great grief and every sort of woe
And widespread sorrow. It became well known
Sadly in songs and stories among men
That Grendel carried on his fight with Hrothgar,
Waging hostilities with murderous raids
For many seasons of continual strife.
He sought no peace with any of the Danes,
Or to stop slaughtering, or come to terms,
Nor could the councillors have any hope
Of compensation at the killer's hands,
But the vile monster carried on his crimes,
The dark death-shadow hovered and attacked
Both young and old, and occupied unseen
The misty moors; it is a mystery
To men where such hell-demons live and move.
    So mankind's enemy, the lonely monster,
Kept on committing violent assaults
And fearful crimes. He dwelt in Heorot
On dark nights, in the decorated hall;
But he could not approach the treasure throne, *
Fulfil that wish; the Lord would not allow it.
    That was great sorrow to the Shilding king,
The breaking of his heart. Many great men
Sat oft in council and deliberated

7

What would be best for the brave-hearted folk
To undertake against these dire attacks.
Sometimes they offered up at pagan shrines *
A sacrifice, and said prayers to the devil,
That he would give them help against the troubles
That terrorised the Danes. Such was their custom,
The hope of heathen men. They thought of hell
Within their hearts, they turned aside from God,
And did not know the Lord, the Judge of deeds,
Nor could they praise the Guardian of heaven,
The Prince of glory. Woe shall come to him
Who casts his soul into the abyss of fire
Through wicked sin, nor trusts in consolation,
Nor mends his ways. Well shall it be for him
Who after dying may approach the Lord
And live in peace within the Father's arms.

III

Beowulf the Geat hears of this,
crosses the sea, and is challenged
by a coastguard.

So Hrothgar's kinsmen seethed with ceaseless care,
Wise men did not know how to end that woe;
The trouble was too strong and fierce and lasting,
That cruel, vicious malice, and that worst
Of night-time fears that fell upon the people.
    A Geatish hero, Hygelac's retainer,
Heard from his home about the deeds of Grendel.
He was the mightiest of mankind in strength
In those days living, powerful and noble.
He ordered a fine ship to be prepared
For him, and said that he would go and visit
That king of warriors, the famous prince,
Across the sea, since he had need of men.
Wise folk did not restrain him from the journey,
Though he was dear to them; they urged him on,
The valiant champion, and checked the omens.
This nobleman had chosen from the Geats
The bravest warriors that he could find.
With fourteen men he went down to the ship,
The skilled seafarer led them to the shore,
And in due time they launched it on the waves,
The boat beside the bank. The eager men
Stepped up onto the deck. The current curled

Against the shore. The seamen carried up
Their trappings to the middle of the vessel,
The gleaming battle-gear; then men cast off
The well-braced boat onto the longed-for journey.
Driven by wind and foaming at the prow,
It passed over the sea just like a bird,
Until at some point on the second day
The round-prowed ship had passed across the sea
Far enough for the sailors to see land,
Cliffs and steep hills and the wide promontories.
The sea was crossed, the journey at an end.
Quickly the Geats stepped up onto the shore
And moored their craft. Their coats of mail resounded,
Their battle-armour; they gave thanks to God
That he had given them an easy voyage.

   Then from the wall the coastguard of the Shildings,
Whose job it was to keep watch from the cliffs,
Saw bright shields being borne across the gangway,
Good warlike armour; curiosity
Consumed his mind, to know who these men were.
At once he rode his horse down to the beach,
This thane of Hrothgar; with his hands he raised
His spear aloft, and spoke in formal tones:
'Who are you warriors, armed and wearing corslets,
Bringing this tall ship here across the sea?
I've been the coastguard, kept watch by the shore
For many years, lest on this Danish strand
Some enemy should land here with a fleet
To do us harm. No warriors before
Have ever disembarked more openly;
And yet you do not know whether the kinsmen
And councillors will give you leave to stay.

I never saw a greater champion
Or man in armour than is one of you.
He's no mere hall-retainer, proudly armed,
Unless his noble countenance belies him,
His fine appearance. Now I have to know
Your origins, before you can proceed
Further into the country of the Danes,
Perchance as spies. So, dwellers from afar,
Seafarers, hear at once my simple question.
It would be best to tell me straight away
Exactly who you are and where you come from.'

IIII

*The coastguard accepts Beowulf and
leads him and his troop to Heorot.*

Immediately the leader of the troop
Replied, and opened up his store of words:
'We are all members of the Geatish race
And hearth-companions of King Hygelac.
My father was well known among the nations,
A noble chieftain; Edgetheow was his name.
He lived to a great age, and all wise men
Will well remember him. We have come here
With loyal minds to seek the son of Halfdane,
Your lord and the protector of this people,
So please show favour to us in your judgement.
We have for your great prince, lord of the Danes,
A strong proposal, which will not remain
Concealed, I think. You know, if it is true
As we have heard related, that some foe,
I don't know who, some secret hostile raider,
Brings terror to the Shildings on dark nights,
With untold damage, violence and slaughter.
I may perhaps, with loyal heart, be able
To offer Hrothgar some advice on this,
How, wise and noble, he might overcome
The fiend, if ever there should come a change,
A remedy to end these baleful cares
And to remove these horrible afflictions,

Or else he may for ever have to bear
Relentless grief and suffering, as long
As his fine hall stands in its lofty place.'
    The coastguard answered, sitting on his horse,
A doughty officer: 'A thoughtful man
Must make a judgement between warriors
By words and deeds as clearly as he can.
This is a loyal troop, I have decided,
And friendly to the ruler of the Shildings.
Collect your weapons and your battle-gear,
And I will guide you. I will also tell
My young retainers to protect your ship
From any enemies, your new-tarred boat
Beside the shore, until that round prowed craft
Once more conveys these well loved sailors home,
Over the water-currents back to Geatland,
Whichever of these brave men shall be granted
To come back safely from the fierce encounter.'
    Then they set off, leaving the boat behind;
The spacious ship stood still upon its ropes,
Firm on its anchor. Images of boars
Adorned with gold shone out above their helmets,
That warlike sign kept life-watch over them.
They hurried on together till they saw
The lofty house, well built and gold-adorned,
For men on earth the building most renowned,
In which the noble king had his abode.
Its brightness shone out over many lands.
The coastguard pointed out the splendid hall,
And showed them how to go directly there,
And then he turned his horse, and said these words:
'It's time for me to go; may God almighty

Preserve you with his grace on your adventure.
Meanwhile I must return back to the sea
To keep my watch for any hostile band.'

V

*The Geatish troop is challenged
by an official, and Beowulf
explains their mission.*

The street was paved, and the path showed the way.
Their hard, hand-woven metal corslets shone,
The gleaming chain-mail sang among their armour
As they approached the hall in battle-gear.
Tired from the voyage, the sailors set their broad
Well-tempered shields against the house's wall.
They sat down on the benches, and the men's
Corslets were clattering, their grey-tipped spears
And other weapons stood piled up together.
That iron-clad troop was honourably armed.
    A courtly officer then asked the men
About their character and who they were:
'Whence do you bring these ornamented shields,
Corslets and helmets armed with face-protectors,
And all this battle armour? I am Hrothgar's
Servant and officer. I never saw
A finer group of men from foreign parts.
I think you come for honour, not as outcasts,
And for good-heartedness have sought out Hrothgar.'
    The brave and noble leader of the Geats
Replied to him, and answered with these words:
'We are retainers from the court of Hygelac.
My name is Beowulf. I wish to tell

The glorious prince, your lord, the son of Halfdane,
Our errand here, if he, so great a man,
Is willing to allow me to address him.'
    Wulfgar replied, he was a Wendel warrior,
His courage was well known to many men,
His wisdom and proficiency in war:
'I will approach the leader of the Danes,
Lord of the Shildings and their treasure-giver,
And ask him as you have requested me,
The glorious prince, about your errand here,
And I will speedily bring back to you
The answer that this great man thinks to give me.'
    He set off quickly to where Hrothgar sat,
Agèd and hoary, with his band of nobles.
Boldly he went until he stood before
The Danish king; he knew the courtly customs.
Wulfgar then formally addressed his patron:
'Visitors have arrived here from afar
Across the waters, people of the Geats.
They give their leader's name as Beowulf,
And have requested that they may have speech
With you, my lord; I pray you, gracious Hrothgar,
That you do not deny them what they ask.
They seem from their equipment to be worthy
Of warriors' respect, and specially
Their leader, who has brought these fighting men
Hither, appears to merit high esteem.'

VI

*Hrothgar authorises the troop's entry,
and Beowulf further describes
their intentions.*

Hrothgar replied, the ruler of the Shildings:
'I knew him well when he was but a boy.
His father was called Edgetheow, to whom
Hrethel the Geat granted his only daughter
In marriage, and his valiant son has now
Come here to us, sought out a friendly lord.
Some sailors who delivered to the Geats
Gifts as a courtesy reported back
That he, a famous fighter, has the grip
Of thirty other men within his hand.
Now holy God has sent him for a favour,
As I believe, to extricate the Danes
From Grendel's terror. To that hero I
Shall offer treasures for his bravery.
Now quickly go and tell the band of kinsmen
To come straight in to see me all together,
And make sure in addition that you tell them
That they are welcome to the Danish people.'
    He went then to the doors and spoke these words:
'My noble lord, the ruler of the Danes,
Has ordered me to tell you that he knows
Your ancestry, and you brave-hearted men
From overseas are welcome to him here.

Now you may enter in your battle-dress
And with your helmets, and go up to Hrothgar;
But let your shields and spears remain outside
To await the outcome of your conversation.'
    The hero stood up, round him many men,
A mighty troop of thanes; some stayed behind
To guard their armour, as the chief commanded.
The warrior led, they hastened in together
Under the roof of Heorot. In his helmet
The brave chief strode till he stood on the hearth.
Beowulf spoke, on him the corslet gleamed,
Its chain-mail finely woven by the smith:
'Hail to you, Hrothgar! I am Hygelac's
Kinsman and servant. I have undertaken
Many great enterprises in my youth.
The business about Grendel was made known
To me in my home country. Seamen say
That this hall, the most excellent of buildings,
Stands idle and unused by anyone
After the light of evening disappears
Below the limits of the sky. My people,
The best and wisest men, advised me then,
King Hrothgar, that I ought to seek you out,
Because they knew my strength and battle-prowess,
Which was revealed to them when I returned,
Covered in blood from conflict, having bound
Five of a tribe of giants and destroyed them;
And in another fight beneath the waves
By night I slew sea-monsters; though I suffered
Serious dangers, I avenged their malice
Against the Geats, and crushed our enemies –
They asked for trouble! Now I hope to do

The same with Grendel, with that monstrous wretch,
That demon, in a one-to-one encounter.
I beg to pray now, leader of the Danes,
Lord of the Shildings, for a single favour;
Do not refuse me, chief of warriors,
Friend of this folk, since I have come thus far,
That I alone, with just my band of men,
This troop of fighters, may cleanse Heorot.
I have heard also that this hateful creature
Scorns to use weapons, in his recklessness.
I renounce therefore – so may Hygelac,
My noble lord, be glad in heart with me –
That I should carry sword or linden wood,
Broad shield to fight, but with my grip alone
Tackle the enemy in mortal combat,
Foe against foe; and there must he whom death
Takes off accept the verdict of the Lord.
If he should win I think that he will wish
To eat without restraint inside the hall
The people of the Geats, as he before
Has often eaten Danish warriors.
You will not need to cover up my head
If death should take me, but the lonely one
Will keep me, stained with gore, carry away
My bloody corpse; the solitary fiend
Will want to taste and greedily consume me,
Staining the moorlands red; you would not have
To worry long about my entertainment!
If battle takes me, send to Hygelac
This best of corslets which protects my breast,
Finest of chain-mail, Hrethel's heirloom, wrought
By Weyland. Fate goes ever as it must.' *

VII

Hrothgar welcomes him, and the
Geats join the Danes at their feast.

Hrothgar replied, protector of the Shildings:
'For former deeds and out of graciousness
You, Beowulf my friend, have sought us out.
Your father brought about the greatest feud:
He was the slayer of Heatholaf
Among the Wulfings. Then he could not dwell
Among the Geatish folk for fear of war.
From there he sought the people of the Danes
Across the rolling of the waves, the Shildings.
I ruled the Danish people at that time,
And in my youth controlled these wide domains,
Likewise the treasure-stronghold of those heroes.
My elder brother Heorogar was dead,
Halfdane's first son, a better man than I!
Later I settled off that feud with payment,
Over the watery ways I sent the Wulfings
Old treasures, he in turn swore oaths to me.
    'It grieves me in my heart to have to say
To any man what harm in Heorot
Grendel has done me with his hostile thoughts
And sudden raids. My hall-troop is diminished,
My band of fighters. Fate has swept them off
By Grendel's terror. God could easily *
Restrain the mad attacker from his deeds.

Full often warriors boasted, drunk with beer
Over their ale-cups, that they would await
Here in the beer-hall battle against Grendel,
Confront him with the terror of their swords.
Then was this mead-hall in the morningtide,
This fine room, stained with gore when daylight came,
The wood of all the benches wet with blood,
The whole hall; I had fewer loyal men
In my dear troop by those that death took off.
Sit now to dinner, let the people know,
Victorious hero, what you have in mind.'
    Then space was made within the drinking-hall
For all the Geatish men to go together;
There the brave-hearted warriors went and sat,
Famed for their prowess. A retainer served them
Who in his hands bore decorated ale-cups
And poured clear mead. Sometimes the minstrel sang
Brightly in Heorot; thus the numerous band
Of Danish men and Geats took their pleasure.

VIII

The Dane Unferth gives a disparaging
account of a swimming contest
between Breca and Beowulf, who
responds with his different version.

Unferth then spoke, he was the son of Edgelaf;
He sat close by the leader of the Shildings,
And planned to make a hostile speech. To him
The journey of the great seafarer Beowulf
Was a hard blow, for he could not accept
That any other man on earth should be
The object of more glory than himself:
'Are you the Beowulf who strove with Breca
Over the wide sea in a swimming match,
When you for daring tested out the currents,
And for a foolish boast both risked your lives
In the deep water; nor could anyone
Dissuade you, friend or foe, from that sad venture?
Then you thrust back the billows with your arms,
Traversed the currents, pushed them with your hands,
Passed through the sea; the ocean seethed with waves,
With wintry surges. You two in the water
Laboured for seven nights, and he out-swam you,
Had greater power. When the morning came
The sea delivered him to Romerike,
From where he went back to his native land,
Dear to his folk, the country of the Brondings,

And the fine fortress where he had his people,
Estate and treasures. All his boast with you
The son of Beanstan totally achieved.
I now expect a less good outcome for you,
Though you have prospered in the rush of battle
And cruel war, if you dare linger here
Through the long night, awaiting Grendel's coming.'
    Beowulf spoke, the son of Edgetheow:
'Lo, my friend Unferth, after drinking beer
You have had much to say regarding Breca
And his achievement. I believe it's true
That I have greater prowess in the sea,
Strength in the waves, than any other man.
We both agreed to that, when we were boys,
And promised – we were both still in our youth –
That we would risk our lives out on the ocean,
And we did as we said. We held bare swords
Hard in our hands when we swam out to sea
So that we could protect ourselves from whales.
He could by no means swim into the waves
Further than me, or faster through the water,
And nor would I leave him; we were together
For five nights in the sea, until the currents,
The surging waves, cold weather, darkening night,
Drove us apart, and the fierce northern wind
Swung round against us; cruel were the billows.
Then were the spirits of the sea-fish raised,
And here my hard, hand-woven corslet helped me,
My twisted chain-mail covering my breast,
Adorned with gold. A hostile creature dragged
Me to the bottom, and there held me fast
Grim in its grip; however, it was granted

That I could pierce the monster with my sword-point,
And so the thrust of battle, through my hand,
Deprived that mighty sea-beast of its life.

VIIII

*The account of the swimming
contest continues, and Hrothgar and
Wealhtheow his queen express hopes
that Beowulf will succeed
in his mission.*

'After that many hostile sea-creatures
Harassed me hard, and with my well-tried sword
I dealt with them in the best way I could.
By no means did those wicked killers get
Their longed-for feast, or make a meal of me,
A banquet at the bottom of the sea,
But in the morning, wounded by my sword,
They lay, cast by the waves up on the shore,
Slain by my weapon, so that from that time
They never hindered any seafarers
At that deep crossing. Light came from the east,
God's beacon bright, the waters settled down,
And I was able then to see the headlands,
The windy sea-walls. Often fate protects
A man who is not doomed, if he is brave.
Thus was it granted me that with my sword
I slew nine water-monsters. I have never
Heard of a tougher fight under the sky
Nor a more hard-pressed warrior in the sea.
Though weary from my journey, I escaped
Alive the clutches of my foes. The currents

And surging billows bore me up ashore
In Finland. I have never heard that you
Have undergone such challenging encounters
Or terrifying fights, and neither Breca
Nor you has done such deeds in battle-play
So bravely with your decorated swords
(I do not want to boast of this too much).
But you became the slayer of your brothers,
Your closest kinsmen, for which sin in hell
You'll suffer torment, clever though you are.
Son of Edgelaf, I tell you for a fact
That Grendel, the vile monster, never would
Have brought your prince such manifold disasters
And harms in Heorot if your heart and spirit
Were as courageous as you rate yourself.
But he has found he has small need to fear
Hostile attacks or sword-fights from your people,
The Battle-Shildings; so he takes his tribute,
And spares no one among the Danish nation,
He does just as he pleases, kills and feasts,
Expecting no resistance from the Danes.
But shortly I propose to offer him
Strife, with the might and valour of the Geats.
Then from tomorrow those who wish to come
And take their mead here should be safe to do so,
When dawn appears over the sons of men,
And the bright sun shines on us from the south.'

   The treasure-giver then was overjoyed,
Grey-haired and famed in war; the Danish prince
Felt confident that help was now at hand.
The nation's guardian saw in Beowulf
Such firm and single-minded steadfastness.

Then there was noisy laughter among men,
Their words were joyful. Hrothgar's queen went forth,
Wealhtheow performed the proper courtesies,
And, gold-adorned, greeted the men in hall.
The noble lady offered first a cup
To the protector of the Danish lands,
Bade him be happy at that beer-drinking,
Dear to his people; he received with joy
Both feast and cup, that king of victories.
The lady of the Helmings then went round
To all the warriors, both young and old,
Offering each a precious cup, until
The moment when the queen, bedecked with rings,
Noble in heart, tendered a cup of mead
To Beowulf, greeted the Geatish prince,
And with wise words thanked God that her desire
Had come to pass, that she could put her trust
In any man for help in their distress.
The war-fierce warrior received that cup
From Wealhtheow, and then, ready for battle,
Beowulf, son of Edgetheow, proclaimed:
'I planned, when I set out onto the waves,
Sat in the sea-boat with my band of men,
That I would either fully bring and pass
Your people's wish, or perish in the fight,
Fast in the clutches of the enemy.
I will achieve a feat of noble valour,
Or spend my last day in this banquet-hall.'
    Then as of old were spoken in that hall
Many brave words. The people were in joy,
With cheerful sound of revelling retainers,
Until the son of Halfdane in due course

Wanted to set off for his night's repose.
He knew the monster planned to raid the hall
After the sun's light was no longer seen
And darkening night came gliding over all,
With shapes of shadows black beneath the clouds.
The whole troop stood up. Hrothgar greeted Beowulf,
Wishing him luck, that he might keep control
Over the wine-hall, and he spoke these words:
'Never have I entrusted any man
Before, since I could raise my hand and shield,
To guard the mighty Danish banquet-hall,
Until I now commit this task to you.
Occupy now and hold this best of houses,
Think about glory, show your bravery,
Keep watch for enemies. You will not lack
For anything you wish if you survive
Alive the outcome of this noble deed.'

X

The Danes retire, leaving the Geats
in charge of Heorot.

Hrothgar went out then with his band of heroes,
The leader of the Shildings from the hall.
The war-chief wished to leave and pass the night
With Wealhtheow, his queen and bed-fellow.
The King of Glory had, as men perceived,
Set up a hall-protector against Grendel,
Whose special office for the Danish prince
Was to keep watch for the marauding giant.
The Geatish lord was fully confident
In his own might and in the Lord's support,
And he took off his iron coat of mail,
His helmet from his head, and gave his sword,
The best of blades, to one of his retainers,
Commanding him to guard his war-equipment.
Then Beowulf, the hero of the Geats,
Spoke words of reassurance to his men
In the great hall, before he went to bed:
'I rate myself no less in battle-prowess
And fighting deeds than Grendel does himself;
Therefore I will not kill him with my sword,
Deprive him of his life, although I could.
He does not know the benefit of weapons
That he might strike me with and hew my shield,
Though he is famous for his deeds of malice;

But we two in the night will do without
Swords, if he dares take on the fight unarmed,
And afterwards wise God, the holy Lord,
Will grant the victory to one of us,
Whichever seems to him appropriate.'
   The brave man lay down then, the pillow held
The warrior's face, and many doughty seamen
Around him sank into their resting places.
None of them thought that he would ever part
From there to see his much-loved home again,
His folk and city where he was brought up,
For they knew well that slaughter had removed
Too many Danes already from that wine-hall.
But truly God had granted to the Geats
His comfort and support, that they should have
Victory in that fight, and that their foe
Should be defeated by their leader's skill
And matchless strength. The truth is clearly shown
That mighty God has always ruled mankind.
   In the black night the prowler in the darkness
Came striding close. The warriors were asleep
Whose job it was to guard the gabled house,
All except one (it was well known to men
That the grim demon could not drag them down
Under the shades without the Lord's consent);
But he, awake, awaited fierce in heart
The outcome of the fight against that terror.

XI

*Grendel attacks, kills a Geat, and is
held in a powerful grip by Beowulf.*

Then from the marshes, under mists of darkness,
Grendel approached; he bore the wrath of God.
The wicked raider planned to capture one
Of humankind within that lofty hall.
Under the clouds he came where he well knew
The wine-house was, the golden hall of men,
Treasure-adorned. That was not the first time
That he had come to visit Hrothgar's home,
But never in his life, before or since,
Did he meet harder luck from hall-retainers.
The joyless creature made his way towards
The building; straightaway the door burst open
As soon as he had touched it with his hands,
Though it was firmly fixed on metal bars.
Then, grim and angry, he swung open wide
Heorot's mouth, and quickly after that
The fierce fiend strode onto the gleaming floor.
An ugly light like fire shone from his eyes.
Inside the hall he looked on many men,
A band of kinsmen sleeping all together,
A troop of warriors, and his spirit laughed;
The evil monster planned, before day came,
To separate the body from the soul
Of one of them, since there appeared before him

The expectation of a plenteous feast.
But fate decreed that following that night
He never more should be allowed to taste
The flesh of men. Hygelac's mighty kinsman
Watched how the evil wretch would execute
His rapid raid. The monster had no wish
To linger, but immediately grabbed
One of the sleeping men, greedily tore him,
Bit through his bones, and drank blood from his veins,
Swallowed great chunks. In no time he consumed
All of the corpse, even its feet and hands.
He strode on further; with his hands he seized
The noble-minded warrior in his bed,
Who instantly caught hold of the intruder
Tightly, and sat up, leaning on his arm.
The criminal was quickly made aware
That he had never, anywhere on earth,
Met with a stronger grip from any man.
He felt the panic rising in his spirit,
But could not break away, although his heart
Was eager to be off, he wished to flee
Into some hiding place, some haunt of devils.
What happened to him there was not the same
As he had met before in all his days.
Hygelac's kinsman brought back to his mind
His earlier evening speech; he stood upright
Gripping him hard, so that his fingers snapped.
The giant tried to leave, the man came with him,
The massive creature wanted, if he could,
To run away from there and flee far off
Into the fens. He clearly felt his fingers
Were firmly in his powerful foe-man's grasp.

That was a sorry journey that the fiend
Had made to Heorot! The noble house
Resounded; every Dane down in the fortress
Where they were cowering, all who heard that din,
Were terrified. The two antagonists
Fought savagely. The building shook with noise.
It was a wonder that the banquet-hall
Survived the battering and did not fall
Down to the ground, but it was skilfully
Crafted with iron struts, and firmly fixed
Inside and out; yet many mead-benches
Adorned with gold were torn up from the floor
Wherever in the room these foes were fighting.
The Shilding councillors had never thought
That it could be destroyed by any man
Of flesh and blood, unless a fire's embrace
Should swallow it in flames. The sounds of strife
Went on continuously, causing terror
To the North Danes, to every one of those
Who from the ramparts heard that hideous howl,
The dreadful song sung by God's adversary
Beaten, as he bewailed his grievous wound,
That captive out of hell. He held him fast
Who was of all mankind the mightiest
Of anybody living at that time.

XII

The fight continues, and Grendel
flees, fatally wounded.

The hero had no wish at any price
To let the killer get away alive,
Nor did he judge his presence in this world
To be of benefit to any man.
There Beowulf's warriors drew their ancient swords,
They hoped to save their lord and master's life,
Protect that glorious prince as best they could.
They did not know, when they joined in the battle,
Those brave and sturdy-hearted warriors,
Meaning to hack at him on every side
And kill him, that no sword, however good,
No weapon in the world, could touch that sinner.
For he had put a spell on battle-weapons,
On every blade. But even so that day
His time on earth would reach its wretched end,
And far off into the domain of fiends
His alien soul was destined to depart.
He then discovered, who before had brought
Much grief of spirit to the human race
By many crimes (he was the foe of God),
That now his body's power would not prevail,
For Hygelac's brave kinsman had his hand
Locked firmly in his grip; each of those two
Meant evil to the other while he lived.

The loathsome monster felt a grievous wound,
A rent was clearly seen upon his shoulder,
His sinews sprang apart, the muscles split.
To Beowulf was granted victory,
And Grendel had to flee, mortally hurt,
Back to the fen-slopes, to his grim abode.
He knew for certain that his life had reached
Its end, the final number of his days.
After that bloody conflict all the Danes
Received their wish; he who from far away
Had come, wise and great-spirited, had cleansed
Hrothgar's great hall, and saved it from attacks.
His night's work pleased him, his heroic deeds;
The Geatish leader had fulfilled his boast
To the East Danes, and also remedied
All the distress and sorrows they had suffered.
And through malign necessity endured,
No little sadness. That was clearly seen
After the battle-brave one fixed the whole
Of Grendel's hand and arm and shoulder up
High on the gable underneath the roof.

XIII

*The Danes celebrate Grendel's defeat;
a court poet sings lays about these
events and about the adventures of the
dragon-slayer Sigemund.*

Then in the morning many warriors
Gathered, I heard, around the treasure-hall.
The chieftains of that folk from far and near
Went down the wide ways to inspect that wonder,
The footprints of the foe. His end of life
Brought no regret to any of the men
Who saw the traces of the vanquished one,
How, weary-spirited departing thence,
Beaten by violence, doomed and put to flight,
He left his bloody tracks along the path
Until he reached the water-monsters' pool.
The water there was seething with his blood,
His hot gore mingled with the surging waves.
Condemned by fate he died, bereft of joys,
Laid down his life within his fen retreat,
His heathen soul; and hell received him there.
 Back from the mere retainers young and old
Joyfully rode their steeds along the track,
Men on white horses; there was Beowulf's
Glory recounted; many often said
That nowhere, south or north, between the seas
Over the spacious earth under the sky

Was there another finer shield-bearer
Than him, or worthier to rule a kingdom.
Yet they by no means criticised their lord,
The great Hrothgar, but *he* was a good king.
Sometimes they made their chestnut horses gallop
Where they considered that the country paths
Were best for riding, and they rode in races.
From time to time one of the king's retainers,
A man well stocked with songs and narratives,
Who knew full many of the ancient stories,
Combined his words in new alliterations.
Skilfully he began to tell the tale
Of Beowulf's exploit, and to relate
The story of his deeds, varying words
Ingeniously. He also told of much   *
That he had heard about the bold adventures
Of Sigemund, and many unfamiliar,
The son of Wals's strifes and widespread journeys
And feuds and other violent encounters
Which were not widely known about by men,
Except for Fitela, his close companion,
To whom he sometimes spoke about such things,
The uncle to his nephew, in the times
When they were comrades in all sorts of conflicts.
They had despatched a number of the race
Of giants with their swords. To Sigemund
Arose no little fame after his death,
Since, fierce in battle, he had killed a dragon,
The keeper of a hoard; the prince's son
Dared risk the danger of that deed alone
(Fitela was not with him at that time)
Under the grey rock, and the outcome was

That his fine sword passed through the wondrous
    serpent
And stuck into the wall; the dragon died.
Then through his noble deed the warrior
Could take possession from that treasure-hoard
Of all he wished. He loaded up his boat,
The son of Wals bore up into the ship
The gleaming treasures; fire consumed the dragon.
   He was the most renowned adventurer,
That first of warriors, among all nations,
For his brave deeds, by which he greatly prospered,
After the might of Heremod declined, *
His valour and his strength. Among the Jutes
He was betrayed into the power of foes
And quickly dealt with. Sorrows had beset him
For far too long; but he had made his people
And all the princes frightened for their lives.
Before that many wise men had deplored
The brave man's escapades, for they had hoped
For help in troubles, that that prince's son
Would prosper and take on his father's role
And justly rule the nation and its treasures,
The stronghold and the kingdom of the heroes,
The homeland of the Shildings. Hygelac's
Kinsman appeared a fairer friend to all
Mankind; but Heremod succumbed to sin.
   The young men rode their horses up and down
The sandy paths, and sometimes raced each other.
The morning sun was hastening on its way.
Many brave warriors went to the high hall
To see the wondrous token, and the king
Himself, the guardian of the treasury,

Stepped out triumphant, with a mighty troop
Known for its excellence, and his queen beside him
Went to the mead-hall with her band of maidens.

XIIII

*Hrothgar and Beowulf address
each other.*

Hrothgar proclaimed – he walked up to the hall,
Stood on the steps and gazed at the steep roof
Adorned with gold, and on it Grendel's hand:
'For this fair sight may thanks at once be made
To God almighty! I have long endured
Hateful affliction at the hands of Grendel.
Ever can God work wonder after wonder.
Not long ago I had no hope at all
That I should ever live to see a cure
For my distress and care, when, stained with blood,
This best of halls stood subject to attacks,
A lasting grief to all the councillors,
Who did not think that they could ever save
The palace of the people from their foes,
From devils and from demons. Now a man
Has, through the might of God, performed the deed
Which none of us was able to accomplish.
Truly the lady who brought forth that son
Into the human race, if she still lives,
Can rightly claim the Lord was gracious to her
In her child-bearing. Beowulf, I now
Wish in my soul to love you as a son;
Let us keep well this new relationship.
You shall not lack in any worldly want

If I have power to grant it. Often I
Have given rich rewards to weaker men,
Less battle-bold, and for less great exploits.
By this deed you have won yourself renown
That will abide for ever. May the Lord
Reward you well, as he has done before!'
   Beowulf spoke, the son of Edgetheow:
'We undertook that fight with great good will,
Daringly risked the might of the unknown.
I wish that you could see the fiend himself,
His slaughtered body. It had been my hope
To hold him firmly grasped until he died,
Gripped by my hands until he lost his life,
And not to let him go; but I could not,
The Lord would not permit me to prevent
The fleeing of my deadly enemy;
He was too strong in making his escape.
And yet he let his hand and arm and shoulder
Remain behind in trying to save his life.
But that will not have gained the wretched creature
Any relief, nor will the evil-doer,
Weighed down by sin, thereby live any longer.
The wound retains him in its fatal grip
Closely confined, and now that sin-stained being
Will have to wait for the great Judgement Day,
And what the good Lord will ordain for him.'
Unferth kept quieter then, the son of Edgelaf,
Boasting no more about his warlike deeds.
The princes gazed up at the lofty roof,
Where by the hero's skill had been attached
The arm and hand and fingers of the fiend;
The tips of all the nails were hard like steel,

The heathen monster's vile and deadly claws.
Everyone said that no fine ancient sword
Of any warrior could have done him harm,
Or hurt the ogre's bloody battle-hand.

XV

*A feast is prepared at which Hrothgar
rewards Beowulf with treasures.*

Orders were issued then that Heorot
Should quickly be prepared and decorated,
And many men and women set to work
To make the wine-hall ready. Tapestries
Adorned with gold shone out from all the walls,
Wonderful sights for those that looked at them.
The splendid building had been badly broken,
All the inside, though bonded with iron clamps,
The hinges split apart. Only the roof
Stayed totally undamaged when the fiend,
Guilty of wicked deeds, set off in flight,
Despairing of his life. It is not easy –
Try it who will! – to dodge one's destiny,
But every son of man who bears a soul,
Each dweller on this earth, will find the spot
Appointed as his final resting place,
Where he will sleep after the feast of life.
    The time had come for Halfdane's son, the king,
To come into the hall, where he intended
To take part in the banquet. I have never
Heard of so many tribesmen celebrating
More honourably with their treasure-giver.
Victorious they settled on the benches,
Rejoicing in the feast; Hrothgar and Hrothulf,

Stout-hearted kinsmen in that lofty hall,
Gladly accepted many a cup of mead.
The great house Heorot was filled with friends;
No Shilding at that time was treacherous.
The son of Halfdane then gave Beowulf
A golden decorated battle-banner
As a reward for victory, and a helmet
And corslet; many saw a famous sword
Adorned with treasure borne before that hero.
Then Beowulf drank from a proffered cup
Within the hall; by no means did he feel
Dishonoured to receive those costly gifts
Before the warriors; I have never heard
Of any lord bestowing four such treasures
Adorned with gold among the mead-benches
On anyone in a more gracious way.
Outside the helmet's crown a crest retained
The head protector, closely wired about,
So that no well-filed battle-hardened sword
Might bring harm to that brave shield-warrior
When he would venture out to fight his foes.
The chieftain then gave orders that eight horses
Be brought into the hall up through the precinct
In plaited gear. On one of them the saddle
Was skilfully adorned with sparkling treasure;
That was the war-seat of the mighty king
When Halfdane's son wished to participate
In sword-play. Never at the battle-front
Where men were slaughtered did the valour fail
Of that most well known chief. The Danish king
Presented all these gifts to Beowulf,
Horses and weapons, bade him use them well.

Thus honourably did the famous prince,
The keeper of the nation's hoard, reward
Those valiant deeds with horses and rich treasures,
That nobody who claims to tell the truth
Could ever blame him for ungenerousness.

XVI

*Hrothgar rewards the other Geats,
and the court poet begins a lay about
a fight at Finnsburg.*

Further to that the lord of warriors
Presented treasures on the mead-benches,
Fine heirlooms, to each one who crossed the sea
With Beowulf, and ordered gold should be
Paid for the one that Grendel wickedly
Had killed; he would have murdered more of them
If the all-knowing God and that man's courage
Had not forestalled that fate. The Lord controlled
The destiny of all, as he still does.
Therefore it's best for everyone to plan
And think ahead; the man who long enjoys
Life in the days of labour in this world
Will pass through many things, both good and bad.
    Music and song were both then heard in turn
Before the battle-leader of the Danes,
The harp was plucked and many a tale was told,
And Hrothgar's minstrel, to delight the hall, *
Declaimed among the mead-benches the tale
Of Finn's retainers, when disaster fell,
And Hnaf the Shilding, hero of the Half Danes,
Was struck down on the Frisian field of slaughter.
    'Hildeburh had no need at all to praise
The good faith of the Jutes. Guiltless, she was

46

Deprived of dear ones in the weapon-play,
Of son and brother. They were doomed to fall,
Wounded by spears; that was a grieving lady.
Hoc's daughter mourned, and not without good cause
When morning came, and she, under the sky,
Could see the slaughtered corpses of the kinsmen
Who were, till then, her greatest joys on earth.
Battle took all Finn's thanes, except a few,
So that he could not in that meeting place
Pursue the fight with Hengest to an end,
Nor crush the remnant of the prince's men.
Instead they offered terms, to give them all
Another hall and throne, which they would share
As equals with the Jutish warriors,
And Finn, Folcwalda's son, at treasure-givings
Would daily honour Hengest's troop of Danes
With just as many rings and golden treasures
As in the beer-hall he would give to cheer
The Frisian folk. They drew up on each side
A firm peace treaty. Finn swore oaths to Hengest
Without reserve, that he would treat with honour
The remnants of his troop, according to
The judgement of his council, and that no one
Should break the truce by word or deed, nor ever
Mention maliciously that, leaderless,
They now were subject to their prince's slayer,
Since need compelled them; and if any Frisian
By hostile speech should call to mind the feud,
The sword's sharp edge should be the arbiter.
  'A pyre was raised up high, and funeral gold
Brought from the hoard. That best of warriors,
The Shilding prince, was ready for the fire.

There at the pyre were clearly to be seen
Numerous blood-stained mail-coats, likewise helmets
With gilt and iron-hard images of boars,
And many noble men destroyed by wounds.
No few died in that slaughter. Hildeburh
Commanded her own son to be committed
On Hnaf's pyre to the flames, his body burned,
And placed upon the fire beside his uncle.
The princess led the mourning, sang laments;
Smoke from the slaughtered rose into the air.
That greatest funeral pyre reached to the clouds,
And roared beside the mound. Their heads dissolved,
The scars burst open, and blood spurted forth
From body wounds. Fire, greediest of spirits,
Consumed all parts of those that lost their lives
In battle there from either nation. Thus
Their glory in this world was brought to nothing.

XVII

*The lay is concluded, and
Wealhtheow speaks, expressing
disingenuously her confidence that
her nephew Hrothulf will look
after her sons in due course.*

'Finn's warriors then set off, bereft of friends,
To Frisia, to their homes and the chief city.
But Hengest still unwillingly remained
With Finn throughout the whole long blood-stained
    winter,
Yearned for his homeland, but he could not venture
To steer his round-prowed ship upon the sea –
The waters surged with storms, strove with the wind,
And winter locked the waves in icy bonds –
Until another year arrived on earth,
As now it does, when gloriously bright
Weathers, as ever, keep their proper season.
Winter was over, fair the face of earth.
Adventurers then set sail, guests from the dwellings,
But Hengest thought much more about revenge
Than sailing home (if he could bring about
A hostile meeting), and he kept in mind
The Jutish warriors. Therefore he did not
Decline his duty when the son of Hunlaf
Placed in his lap the sword called Battle-light,
Best of all swords; its edges were well known

Among the Jutes. So cruel death by sword
Befell brave-hearted Finn at his own home,
After Guthlaf and Oslaf came by sea
And spoke with grief about the fierce attack,
And blamed him for their woe. They could no longer
Contain the seething spirit in their breasts.
Then was the hall stained red with blood of foes,
And Finn was slain, the king among his troop,
And also Hildeburh the queen was seized.
The Shilding warriors carried to their ships
All the rich trappings and the precious gems
That they could find at King Finn's dwelling place.
They bore his noble wife away to Denmark,
On a sea-journey, took her to her people.'
   The lay was sung, the minstrel's tale was ended.
The revelry resumed, and sounds of joy
Rose loudly from the benches; cupbearers
Took round the wine in decorated flagons.
Wealhtheow came forth in her golden collar
To where the two great princes sat together,
Uncle and nephew; there was still then peace   *
Between them, each was loyal to the other;
And likewise Unferth, the king's orator,
Sat at the leader of the Shildings' feet.
Everyone trusted in his noble spirit
And heart, though he had not been merciful
Towards his kinsmen in the play of swords.
   The gracious lady of the Shildings spoke:
'Accept this cup, my lord, giver of treasure;
Be in good spirits, speaking to the Geats
With friendly words, as all of us should do.   †
It has been said that you wish to adopt

This hero as your son. Heorot is cleansed,
The gleaming treasure-hall. May you enjoy
Dispensing precious gifts for just as long
As you are able to, until the time
When, at your fated hour, you must go forth,
Leaving your folk and kingdom to your kinsmen.
I know my gracious Hrothulf will with honour
Protect the young men, if you, Shilding lord,
Depart this life before him. I am sure
He will repay with generosity
Our children, if his memory recalls
All that we did to please and honour him
In former times when he was but a child.'

   She went to where her sons were on the bench,
Hrethric and Hrothmund, with the sons of heroes,
The young troop all together; there too sat
Beowulf of the Geats beside the brothers.

XVIII

Wealhtheow gave Beowulf a valuable collar, which Hygelac later had with him during his disastrous raid into Frankish territory, where it was lost to the enemy. Many Danes settle down for the night in Heorot.

A cup was borne to him, and friendly words
Exchanged, and twisted gold bestowed on him.
Two bracelets, corslet, rings, the fairest collar
That I have ever heard of in the world.
I know of no more marvellous adornment
Under the heavens after Hama bore *
The Brosing necklace to the mighty city,
Those jewels richly set, as he was fleeing
The treacherous attacks of Eormenric,
And chose to lead instead a life of virtue.
That collar Hygelac the Geat took with him, †
Grandson of Swerting, on his final journey,
When underneath his banner he defended
His spoils of war and treasure. Fate destroyed him
When he sought trouble through his arrogance
In battle with the Frisians. He bore off
Those wondrous precious stones across the sea,
The mighty prince; he died beneath his shield.
The king's corpse passed into the Frankish power,
Together with his armour and this collar.

Less worthy warriors plundered the dead bodies
After the carnage, and the Geatish corpses
Covered the battlefield. The hall resounded
With cheers. Then Wealhtheow spoke before that
   troop:
  'Enjoy this collar, my dear Beowulf,
You should make good use also of the corslet
And all these treasures; may you greatly prosper,
Using your power, and be to these young boys
A kindly teacher, and I will reward you.
What you have done ensures that far and near
Men will esteem your memory for ever,
Even as widely as the windswept sea
Surrounds the coasts. As long as you have life,
Prince, may you flourish in prosperity,
And in good fortune may you ever be
Supportive in your dealings with my son.
Here all the warriors are mild in spirit,
True to each other, loyal to their lord,
The thanes harmonious and all the people
Ready to serve; and all this band of men
Here at the banquet do as I request.'
   She went then to her seat. That was the best
Of feasts, and all the warriors drank much wine.
They did not know what grim fate had ordained
(As it has often done for many men)
After night came, and Hrothgar had departed
To take his rest elsewhere in his abode.
Numerous warriors occupied the hall,
As they had often done in days gone by.
They cleared away the benches and the space
Was filled throughout with bedding and with bolsters;

But one of the beer-drinkers who prepared
Himself for bed that night was doomed to die.
They placed their battle-shields behind their heads,
And on the benches above every man
High helmets could be seen and chain-mail corslets,
And also mighty spears; it was their custom
Always to be in readiness for battle,
Whether at home or out on active service,
Or any other time when their liege lord
Had need of them; that was a noble nation.

XVIIII

Grendel's mother attacks Heorot and kills a Dane.

They went to sleep. One of them sorely paid
For his night's rest, as often had occurred
When Grendel visited the treasure-hall,
Committing crimes, until his end had come,
His death after his sins. It was revealed
And shown to men that an avenger still
Was living after all that lengthy time
Of violence and trouble. Grendel's mother,
A female monster, suffered piercing grief;
She was a member of that wretched race
That had to dwell in dismal watery places,
Cold hostile streams, after the time when Cain
Became the killer of his only brother;
Guilty and stained by murder he departed
Fleeing the joys of men, and went to dwell
In desert places, and from him descended
Many doomed spirits, one of whom was Grendel,
A hateful ravager who found at Heorot
A watchful warrior waiting for a fight.
The monster tried to take him in its grip,
But he was mindful of his mighty strength,
The ample gift that God had granted him,
And he had faith in the Almighty's grace,
Help and support; therefore he overcame

The foe, and laid to rest the spirit from hell.
Thence mankind's enemy departed, abject,
Deprived of joy, to seek his place of death.
His mother then, greedy and grim in spirit,
Was moved to set off on that grievous journey
And to exact revenge for her son's death.

   She came to Heorot, where the band of Danes
Was sleeping round the hall, and there at once
There came a change of fortune for those men
When Grendel's mother forced her way inside.
She was less frightening to the extent
That female strength, the fighting power of women,
Is not as great as that of men in arms
When the clasped sword, forged by the hammer, sharp
Of blade and stained with blood strikes at the boar
Above the helmet of the opposing foe.
There in the hall was many a hard-edged sword
Drawn from above the benches, many shields
Held firm in hand; they did not pause for helmets
Or corslets when that terror burst upon them.
She was in haste and anxious to get out
And save her life once she had been perceived,
But she had quickly grabbed one of the nobles
And gripped him as she set off for the fen.
The man that she had murdered in his bed
Had ranked as a companion, and had been
The most well loved by Hrothgar of his men,
A powerful and famous warrior.

     Beowulf was not there. Another lodging
Had been appointed for the glorious Geats
After the treasure-giving. There was uproar
In Heorot. She bore the bloody hand

Away with her, and sorrow was renewed
In that abode. It was a poor exchange
By which each side paid with the loss of friends.
    Then the wise king, the agèd warrior,
Grieved sorely in his heart when he had heard
That his chief thane, the dearest of his friends,
Was dead and lifeless. Beowulf was fetched
At once, the famous hero, to his chamber;
At dawn of day the noble champion
Went with his men to where the wise man waited,
Wondering if Almighty God would ever
Bring him relief after this woeful news.
The honoured soldier strode across the floor
With his picked troop – the wooden hall resounded –
So that he could address the Danish lord
And ask if he had had a pleasant night.

XX

*Hrothgar expresses grief at this new
attack, and describes the place where
the monsters live.*

Hrothgar, protector of the Shildings, spoke:
'Ask not of pleasant nights! Grief is renewed
Among the Danish people. Dead is Ashhere,
Yrmenlaf's elder brother and my comrade
And councillor, my bosom arms-companion
While in the heat of battle we protected
Our heads when fighting armies clashed together,
And swords struck boar-defended helmets. Such
A warrior should be, a noble prince,
As Ashhere was. Now a marauding killer
Has foully murdered him in Heorot.
I do not know where this vile creature went,
Pleased with her prey and glorying in her feast.
She has avenged the violent act by which
Grendel was slain in your unyielding grip
Who for too long destroyed and harmed my people.
Guilty, he lost his life in an attack,
And now another mighty ravager
Has come to take revenge for her dead kinsman
And has with fell effect pursued the feud,
As can be seen by very many thanes
Who grieve in spirit for their treasure-giver,
A terrible distress. Now he has died

Who generously would give you all you wished.
    'Among my people I have heard it said,
By countrymen and councillors in hall,
That they have seen two creatures such as this
Haunting the moors, two mighty wasteland-dwellers,
Alien spirits. One of them, they said,
As far as they could tell was like a woman,
The other wretched creature trod the paths
Of exile in the likeness of a male,
But he was bigger, far, than any man.
In times of old the rustics called him Grendel;
They did not know if he had had a father,
Or whether any such mysterious being
Had ever lived before him. They inhabit
The woody headlands, the abodes of wolves,
The wild fen-country, where a waterfall
Pours out into the murk beneath the cliffs
Down from the land. It is not far away
From here, measured in miles, that lies that pool.
Frost-covered woods and firmly rooted trees
Stretch out their branches, darkening the water.
There each night may be seen a dreadful wonder,
Fire on the water. There is no wise man
Alive who's ever visited that spot.
Even a stag exhausted by the hounds,
A strongly antlered hart, seeking the woods,
Chased from afar, would rather lose his life
Beside the pool than that he should plunge in
To save himself. That's not a pleasant place!
When violent storms are stirred up by the wind,
Dark surging waves rise up towards the clouds
Till the sky blackens and the heavens weep.

'Now the decision is for you alone.
You must decide; you do not know the place,
The horrible abode where you may find
The sinful wretch; go, seek it if you dare.
I will reward you for the fight with gifts
And ancient treasures, as I did before,
With twisted gold, if you come back alive.'

XXI

*Beowulf undertakes to attack the new
monster, and they set off towards the
mere. Unferth lends Beowulf
a famous sword.*

Beowulf spoke, the son of Edgetheow:
'Grieve not, wise king! It's best for any man
To avenge his friend rather than greatly mourn him.
To each of us will surely come an end
Of life in this world; let whoever can
Win glory while he lives; that is the best
That any warrior can leave behind him,
An honoured reputation after death.
Rise, keeper of the kingdom, let us hurry
And follow up the track of Grendel's kinsman.
I promise you that he will not escape *
Either into the bosom of the earth
Or in the mountain's woods or ocean's depths,
Wherever he may go. This day be patient
In all your troubles, as I know you will.'
    The old man leapt up and said thanks to God,
The mighty Lord, for what the hero said.
A horse with braided mane was then prepared
For Hrothgar; he rode out in stately style.
A troop of foot-soldiers marched forth beside him.
Her tracks along the forest paths were clear
To see, her passage through the countryside,

As she had moved over the murky moor
Bearing the soulless body of the best
And chief of the retainers who with Hrothgar
Attended to the welfare of the court.
The son of princes then went forth along
The steep stone slopes, the single-passage paths,
The narrow tracks and unfamiliar ways,
High-rising headlands, homes of many sea-beasts.
He went ahead, examining the country,
With a few wise retainers, till he saw
Suddenly mountain-trees leaning across
The pale grey rocks, a forest filled with gloom;
Below lay water, bloody and disturbed.
It was a painful sorrow in their hearts
For all the loyal vassals of the Shildings,
The many thanes and all the noblemen,
When they found Ashhere's head up on the sea-cliff.
The waters foamed with blood and surged with gore;
The men looked on. At times the strident horn
Sang out its call to arms. The troop sat waiting.
They saw across the water many serpents
And strange sea-dragons swimming; and above
Lay other monsters on the rocky slopes,
Such as make sudden sallies in the mornings
Bringing distress to travellers at sea,
And also snakes and fierce wild animals;
But when they heard the war-horn sing out loud,
They rushed away, enraged and furious.
A Geatish archer with an arrow took
The life of one among the tossing waves,
When its sharp point transfixed him fatally;
He swam more slowly through the mere when death

Took hold of him, and quickly in the water
He was hemmed in with barbed boar-hunting spears,
Savagely hooked, and dragged up on the shore;
The men gazed with amazement at that weird
Wave-dweller, at that strange and gruesome beast.
   Beowulf then put on his battle-gear;
He was by no means frightened for his life.
His broad hand-woven corslet, cunningly
Adorned, which had the power to protect
His body and prevent an angry foe's
Malicious grasp from threatening to kill him,
Must now be put on trial beneath the water;
He wore a gleaming helmet on his head,
In which to stir the bottom of the mere,
Pass through the surging currents; it was circled
With shining bands, adorned with precious metals,
Just as the weapon-smith in ancient days
Had crafted it, with images of boars,
So that no blade or battle-sword thereafter
Could bite and cut it. But by no means least
Of all the fighting gear that he took with him
Was a fine hilted sword which, in his need,
Was lent to him by Hrothgar's orator.
Its name was Hrunting, and it was among
The very best of all the old-time treasures;
Its blade was steel, tempered and damascened,
Hardened by blood in battle; it had never
Failed any fighter who had wielded it
When daring to embark on risky ventures
In foreign lands; that was not the first time
That it should take part in a deed of valour.
Unferth, the son of Edgelaf, had forgotten,

The mighty man, the words that he had spoken
Before when drunk with wine, but now he lent
This weapon to the better warrior.
He did not dare himself to risk his life
Under the tumult of the waves, perform
That act of courage; there he lost his chance
Of winning honour by heroic deeds.
But it was not so for the other man
After he had prepared himself for strife.

XXII

Diving into the mere, Beowulf comes
to a strange hall, in which he fights
Grendel's mother. The sword
fails him.

Beowulf spoke, the son of Edgetheow:
'Do not forget, wise prince and famous kinsman
Of Halfdane, patron generous to men,
Now that I am about to take the plunge,
The words we previously spoke together,
That if I, at your need, should lose my life,
You would remain even when I am gone
In the position of a father to me.
Be a protector to my thanes and comrades
If battle takes me; send to Hygelac,
Dear Hrothgar, all the treasures that you gave me.
Then may the Geatish lord, the son of Hrethel,
See well when looking on that golden bounty
That I had found myself a generous
Giver of treasure while I could enjoy it;
And let Unferth, the far-famed warrior,
Retain possession of this ancient heirloom,
This finely patterned and sharp-bladed sword.
With Hrunting I intend to win myself
Great honour, or, if not, then death will take me.'
    After these words the leader of the Geats
Quickly set off, not waiting for an answer.

The surges of the mere received the prince.
He swam down through the water for some time
Before he saw the bottom of the pond.
At once she who for half a hundred years
Had occupied the compass of that pool,
Greedy and grim and fiercely ravenous,
Perceived that from above some man had come
Exploring in the land of alien creatures.
She grabbed at him, and in her gruesome claws
Tight gripped him, but by that she did not harm
His body; his chain-mail protected him,
So that her grisly fingers could not pierce
The corslet's close-linked rings. The she-wolf then,
Descending to the bottom of the mere,
Carried the princely hero to her home,
Holding him so that he could not wield weapons
Despite his mighty strength, while many strange
Creatures attacked him in the deep, sea-beasts
Stabbed at his battle-armour with their tusks,
Monsters oppressed him. Then the hero saw
That he was in some fearful sort of hall
Where water could no longer bother him,
No sudden rush of waves beneath its roof;
And he could see the bright light from a fire.

   He looked upon the monster of the deep,
The mighty sea-wife; with the sword he struck,
Restraining not the stroke, and on her head
The blade rang out its greedy song of war.
But at that point the visitor found out
That the great sword had lost the power to bite
And harm her life; its famous edge had failed
The prince at need. Before that it had suffered

Many encounters, often cleft the helmet
Or chain-mail of the doomed; that was the first
Time the fine weapon let its wielder down.

    Hygelac's kinsman still stayed resolute,
Mindful of greatness, he by no means let
His courage falter. Then the angry man
Cast down that jewelled sword onto the ground,
So that it lay there with its strong steel blade.
Instead he put his trust in his own strength
And hand-grip. That is what a man must do
If he intends to win long-lasting glory
In war; he must not care about his life.
The Geatish chieftain grasped her by the shoulder,
The monster's mother, relishing the fight;
Enraged and battle-hardened he threw down
His mortal foe and flung her to the floor;
But quickly she repaid him when she grabbed
At him, and held him with her vicious claws.
Weary in spirit that strongest warrior
Stumbled and fell. At once she held him down,
The stranger in her hall, and drew her dagger,
Broad and bright-edged; she meant to avenge her son,
Her only offspring. On his shoulder lay
His close-linked corslet, and it saved his life,
Blocking the entrance of both point and edge.
Edgetheow's son, the Geatish champion,
Would then have passed away in that deep place
If his mail-coat had not protected him,
His hardy armour, and the holy Lord
Had not controlled the victory; wise God
Settled the outcome justly, as he does
In every case. The hero found his feet.

XXIII

Finding a larger and better sword,
Beowulf kills Grendel's mother
and decapitates Grendel's corpse.
He returns to the anxiously waiting
Geats bearing Grendel's head,
which they carry back to Heorot.

Then suddenly among a stack of weapons
He saw an ancient sword, the work of giants,
Of finest tempered steel, with strong, sharp edges,
Which any warrior would be proud to own.
It was undoubtedly the best of weapons,
But bigger far than any other man
Would have the strength to carry into battle.
Raging and desperate he seized its hilt,
Despairing of his life unsheathed its blade,
And furiously struck, so that the edge
Bit hard into the neck, severed the bone
And passed completely through the fated flesh.
She fell down to the floor; the sword dripped blood;
The hero was delighted by his work.
  The light shone out more brightly from the fire,
Even as the candle of the sky shines down
From heaven. He looked around the hall and moved
Along the wall. The thane of Hygelac
Raised up the weapon firmly by the hilt,
Angry and resolute. That ancient sword

Proved far from useless to the warrior,
Since he intended forthwith to repay
Grendel for all the many violent raids
That he had made upon the Danish race,
Many more times than on that first occasion
When he slew Hrothgar's comrades in their sleep,
Consuming fifteen of the Danish men,
And carried off an equal number with him,
A loathsome spoil. He paid him back for that,
The angry fighter, when he came across
The lifeless Grendel lying on a bed,
Finished with warfare, as that final fight
At Heorot had hurt him fatally.
When it received a blow his corpse bounced up,
A hefty sword-stroke, which cut off his head.

    After a while the men that waited there
With Hrothgar looking at the water's surface
Saw that the surging waves were mixed with blood.
The grey-haired veterans then conferred together
About the hero, but with little hope
He would come back, triumphant and victorious,
To seek the famous prince; it seemed to many
That the sea-monster had defeated him.
The ninth hour came. The Shildings left the headland,
The country's ruler set off to go home.
The visitors remained there, sick at heart,
Staring disconsolately at the mere.
They wished, without much hope, that they might see
Their much-loved lord returning from the depths.

    Meanwhile that sword, soaked in the monster's blood,
Began to fade away like icicles
In warmth; it was a truly wondrous thing

That it entirely melted, just as ice
Does, when the Father frees the bonds of frost,
Unwinds the binding fetters of the flood,
He who controls the seasons and the times,
The very God. The leader of the Geats
As he was leaving did not carry off
Anything from that place except the head,
Together with the hilt adorned with jewels,
Although he saw there many other treasures;
The patterned blade had melted and burnt up,
Such was the heat and venom of the blood
Of the strange monster who had died therein.
Then he who had survived that mortal combat
Immediately thrust up through the water.
Now that the alien spirit had left this life,
Departed from this transitory world,
The tumult of the waves had settled down
In the broad pool. The leader of the seamen
Came swimming powerfully back to land,
Rejoicing in the burden he bore with him,
The booty from below. His troop of men
Hastened at once to meet him, thanking God,
Joyful to see the prince alive and whole.
They quickly took his helmet from his head
And loosed his corslet. Underneath the clouds
The water, red with bloody gore, grew still.

    They set off on the footpaths, glad at heart,
Passed through the country on the well-known road
Triumphantly, but those who bore the head
Back from the sea-cliff found it heavy work,
Strong though they were. It needed four of them
To bring the head of Grendel on a spear-shaft

Up to the gold-hall; and at last that troop
Of fourteen war-bold Geats reached Heorot,
Their brave lord marching with them through the
    meadows.
The great and glorious leader of the thanes,
He who had triumphed in that heroism,
Advanced into the hall and greeted Hrothgar.
Then Grendel's head was carried by the hair
Onto the hall floor where the men were drinking,
Before the nobles, with the queen among them,
A horrible and terrifying sight
For them to look at; everybody stared.

XXIIII

Beowulf describes his encounter,
and Hrothgar replies at length.

Beowulf spoke, the son of Edgetheow:
'Great son of Halfdane, ruler of the Shildings,
With joyful hearts we have brought back for you
This booty from the sea which you see here,
A token of success. I risked my life
In no small way in strife beneath the water,
And at great hazard undertook that deed.
The combat might have ended straight away
Without God's help. With Hrunting I could not
Defeat my foe, fine weapon though it was;
But the Almighty ruler granted me,
The constant guide of those who strive alone,
That I saw hanging splendid on the wall
A mighty ancient sword, and I was able
To draw that weapon. Thus I had the chance
In the ensuing struggle to destroy
The guardian of the house, and after that,
Suffused with blood, with hottest battle-gore,
The patterned blade dissolved and burnt away.
From the fiends' lair I carried off its hilt.
I have avenged their criminal assaults,
The killings of the Danes, as it was fitting.
I now assure you that your band of men
Can safely sleep without anxiety,

With you and all your folk in Heorot,
Both young and old; you need no longer fear,
Prince of the Shildings, as you did before,
The constant threat to life experienced
From that vile kindred by your warriors.'
 Then was the golden hilt placed in the hands
Of the old man, the grey-haired general,
The ancient work of giants; after the fall
Of those two fiends that work of master-craftsmen
Came to the keeping of the Danish king,
And when the violent enemy of God,
Guilty of murder, and his mother too,
Went from this world, it passed into the keeping
Of the best king who ruled between the seas
Among all those in Scandinavia
Who shared out treasure to their loyal subjects.
 Hrothgar replied, looking upon that hilt,
The old heirloom, on which had been engraved
The onset of the strife in ancient times *
When overwhelming waters of the flood
Fell on the race of giants and destroyed them.
That tribe was hostile to the eternal Lord;
The Ruler rendered them that retribution
Of surging billows. All this was set down
And clearly told in rune-staves on the guard-plates
In purest gold, inscribed there for whoever
That damascened sword with its twisted hilt
Was first created for. The wise man spoke,
The son of Halfdane – everyone was silent:
 'As an old monarch who has always tried
To promote truth and right among these subjects,
And well recalls our nation's history,

I feel myself entitled to declare
This noble man a better man than I am.
Your glory, my friend Beowulf, is assured
Throughout the wide ways, among every race.
I have no doubt you will maintain this might
Steadily, with the wisdom of your spirit.
I will continue in close friendship with you,
As we agreed before. You will become
A lasting consolation to your people,
Help for the heroes. Heremod was not
Such for the Danes; he did not bring about
What they desired, but rather he provoked
Slaughter and carnage for the Shildings' people.
When angered he would kill his fellow-diners,
His closest comrades, till he went alone
In exile from the company of men,
That famous prince. Although Almighty God
Had raised him up to have the benefits
Of strength and power above all other men,
There grew a blood-lust in his mind and breast.
He did not share out treasures to the Danes,
Rewarding them for merit. So he lived
Joyless, and suffered torment for the strife
And lasting sorrow he had caused his subjects.
Be warned by this, and keep to manly virtues.
I, old and wise, tender you this advice.

   'It is a wondrous thing to contemplate
How mighty God, with his all-seeing mind,
Shares out among men wisdom, land and rank.
He holds dominion over everything.
Sometimes he lets the spirit of a man
Of a great family live in happiness,

And grants him earthly joy in his own land
To be commander of a fortress-city,
Gives him control of regions of the world,
Rule which he wrongly thinks will never end.
He dwells in plenty; sickness and old age
Afflict him not at all, no anxious cares
Darken his spirit, no hostilities
Drive him to war, and everything on earth
Happens exactly as he would desire;
He seems to be immune from all misfortune, . . .

XXV

*Hrothgar continues his speech,
and they retire for the night.
Next morning Beowulf returns
Unferth's sword. The Geats are
keen to return home.*

Until a certain arrogance is born *
And grows in him; the guardian of his soul,
Its warden, dozes and too deeply sleeps,
His mind on other cares; meanwhile the killer
Is near at hand and shooting from his bow.
His head may wear a helmet, but his breast
Beneath is smitten by a bitter shaft;
He is unable to protect himself
From the perverse enticements of the devil.
What he had long possessed now seems to him
Too little, and, becoming covetous,
No longer does he share out golden rings
In honourable style to his retainers,
Forgetting and not caring for his fate,
Because God earlier had granted him
The glorious Lord, a goodly share of honour.
The end will come, the transitory body
Fated to die will fail and fade away.
Another will take over and share out
Without regret the treasures of this prince,
His splendid heirlooms, with no sense of fear.

Protect yourself from such death-dealing hate,
Dear Beowulf, you best of men, and choose
The better way, of virtue leading to
Eternal life. Do not succumb to pride,
Great hero; now the glory of your might
Will flourish for a while, but soon enough
Sickness or sword will part you from your strength,
Or the embrace of fire, or surge of flood,
Or sharpness of a blade, or flight of spear,
Or sad old age; the brightness of your eyes
May fade and darken; in due course of time,
Most noble warrior, death will overcome you.
   'For half a hundred years beneath the clouds
I ruled the Danes, protecting them in war
With spears and swords throughout this middle-earth
From many tribes, until I felt I had
No foes beneath the compass of the sky.
But then, alas, a change came to my land,
Grief after joy, when Grendel, ancient foe,
Began to mount attacks; and ceaselessly
Throughout his persecution I have suffered
Great trouble in my heart. The Lord be thanked,
Eternal God, that I have stayed alive
Long enough for my eyes to have the chance
Of looking on his battle-bloodied head
After the lasting strife. Go to the bench,
And, honoured by your feat, enjoy the feast.
Tomorrow morning we will talk again,
And many treasures will be passed between us.'
   The Geat was glad at heart, and went at once
To find his place as the wise man had bidden.
Then as before another splendid banquet

Was served to all those brave men in the hall.
When the dark cloak of night covered the land
The troops rose to their feet. The grey-haired prince,
The agèd Shilding, wished to go to bed,
As did the gallant Geatish champion,
Tired beyond measure after his exertions.
Straightway a thane, appointed to look after
The hero who had come from far away,
Now weary from his fighting, led him forth
And courteously saw to all his needs,
As in those days befitted such a seaman.

So, brave in heart, he took his rest. The hall
Stood towering high, broad and adorned with gold.
Nearby the guest slept soundly, till the black
Blithe-hearted raven heralded the joy
Of heaven, and the sun came shining bright
Across the shadows. Warriors woke up,
Nobles were keen to gather with their people;
But he, the valiant-hearted visitor,
Was eager to return and board his ship
And journey far away to his own land.

The hero bade Unferth, the son of Edgelaf,
To take possession of his sword again,
The treasured Hrunting, thanked him for the loan,
Said that he judged it a good friend in war,
Mighty in battle; he did not disparage
Its blade at all, he was a gracious man.
His warriors, having got their armour ready,
Were eager to be off; their prince, esteemed
Among the Danes, went to the raised floor where
The noble ruler of the land was sitting,
And there the valiant hero greeted Hrothgar.

XXVI

Beowulf and Hrothgar exchange
speeches, and more treasures are
given to Beowulf.

Beowulf spoke, the son of Edgetheow:
'Now we seafarers from our distant land
Are eager to return to Hygelac.
We have been dealt with here and entertained
As well as we could wish, and you yourself
Have treated us with magnanimity.
If there is anything that I can do
To earn more of your love by deeds of war
Than I have so far done, I shall at once
Be ready. If I hear across the sea
That any of your neighbours threaten you,
As enemies have sometimes done before,
I will bring here a thousand warriors
To help you. Although Hygelac is young,
The Geatish king and guardian of the people,
I know that he will give me his support
In word and deed that I should honour you
And bring you help with spears and force of arms
When you have need of men. And if your son,
The princely Hrethric, should decide to come
And sojourn with us at the Geatish court,
He will find many friends there. It is good
For men of worth to visit far-off lands.'

Hrothgar then spoke and gave him this reply:
'Wise God has put these sayings in your mind.
I never heard a young man speak so sagely.
You are both strong in might and wise in spirit,
A speaker of sound words. In my opinion,
If chance of battle or if spear or sword
Or illness should deprive the son of Hrethel,
Your prince, of life, and you are still alive,
The Sea-Geats could not find a better man
To choose as king, as keeper of their treasures,
If you were willing to command that kingdom.
The more I know of you the more I love you,
Dear Beowulf, for you have made it sure
That peace shall last between the Geats and Danes,
Our nations, and hostility and strife
Which at one time they suffered shall be stilled.
As long as I shall rule this spacious realm,
All treasures shall be shared between our peoples
And gifts exchanged over the gannet's bath;
The ring-prowed ships shall bring across the sea
Presents and other tokens of affection.
I know our nations now are firmly bound
Together in our dealings with both friend
And foe, and with no guile between the two
As used to be the case in former times.'
    Then Halfdane's kinsman, leader of the army,
Gave him within the hall twelve precious treasures,
Bidding him with these gifts to make his way
Home safely through the sea to his dear tribe,
And said he hoped that he would come back soon.
The high-born king, the ruler of the Danes,
Warmly embraced that best of thanes and kissed him,

While tears fell from the grey-haired Shilding's eyes.
The wise old ruler thought it was more likely
That they would never after meet again.
So dear to him this warrior had become
That he could not restrain his breast's emotions,
For in his heart and in his private thoughts
There burned a deep affection for this man.

    Beowulf, then, replete with golden gifts,
The champion, victorious with his treasures,
Departed thence over the grassy land.
The ship at anchor waited for its owner.
They greatly praised the generosity
Of Hrothgar as they went. In every way
He was a blameless king, until old age,
As is its way, deprived him of his power.

XXVII

*The Geats go to the sea,
the coastguard is rewarded,
and they sail home. Hygelac's nearby
home is mentioned, and his queen
Hygd praised and contrasted
with Offa's queen.*

The troop of brave young soldiers reached the sea,
Wearing their armour with their chain-linked corslets.
The coastguard saw the warriors returning
As he had watched before when first they landed.
From the hill top he did not greet those men
With fierceness, but he rode at once towards them
And said the Geatish warriors in their armour
Were welcome as they journeyed to their ship.
There on the shore the broad-beamed boat was loaded,
The ring-prowed ship, with all their battle-gear,
The treasures and the horses, and the mast
Towered above the gifts from Hrothgar's hoard.
Beowulf gave the keeper of the boat
A sword adorned with gold, so that thereafter
He was more honoured on the mead-benches
By virtue of that valuable heirloom.
    The hero then departed on his ship,
Which stirred up the deep waters, leaving Denmark.
They hoisted up the sail beside the mast
And tied it firmly; the ship's timbers groaned.

Over the waves the wind propelled the boat,
With foamy neck it sailed across the waters,
The well-made craft surged through the briny currents
Until they could descry the cliffs of Geatland,
The well-known headlands. Driven by the breeze
The boat pressed up and stood against the shore.
The harbourmaster straightaway arrived
At the land's edge, he who for long had watched
And waited eagerly beside the coast
For the return of those beloved men.
He tied the broad-beamed boat up to the bank,
Firm on its anchor-cables, lest the power
Of waves should drive the wooden craft away.
He ordered men to unload the nobles' treasures,
Gold plate and ornaments; it was not far
From there to seek the giver-out of bounty,
Hygelac, son of Hrethel, where he dwelt
At home with his companions near the sea.
The house was splendid; in that high hall reigned
The king, a valiant figure of a man,
And Hygd, daughter of Hareth, the young queen,
Wise and accomplished, though she had not lived
For very many years within the court.
She was a gracious lady to the Geats,
Benevolent and generous of gifts.

   Thryth, on the other hand, the well known queen, *
Was moved by arrogance to heinous sins;
None of that loyal retinue would dare,
However brave, to set their eyes upon her,
Or if one did he could expect tight bonds
Of twisted rope to hold him, while a sword
Was sent for which would swiftly end his life.

But it is not fit practice for a queen,
However beautiful, to bring about
The execution of a loyal man
For an imagined insult; better far
That she should be an influence for peace.
So Offa quickly put a stop to that;
According to the stories told in beer-halls
She gave up injuring and harming people
As soon as, gold-adorned, she was betrothed
To the young champion, the noble hero,
And at her father's bidding made the journey
Across the yellow flood to Offa's hall.
Thereafter on the throne she lived a life
Famous for virtue, cherished with great love
That prince of heroes, who, as I have heard,
Was best of all mankind between the seas
Among the human race. For warlike deeds
And generosity Offa was held
In honour far and wide, and wisely ruled
His kingdom. From their union was born
Eomor, leader in due course of heroes,
Grandson of Garmund, powerful in war.

XXVIII

The troop are greeted by Hygelac and
Hygd, and Beowulf begins an account
of his recent adventures, digressing
to forecast trouble ahead between
the Danes and Heathobards.

The brave man then departed with his troop,
Marching across the foreshore, as the sun,
The candle of the world, shone from the south.
They set off on their journey, urgently
Pressed on, until they came to where they knew
Their warrior prince, slayer of Ongentheow,
Would be dispensing treasure in his city,
The young war-king. That Beowulf had landed *
Was instantly announced to Hygelac,
And that the leader of the warriors,
His arms-companion, had returned alive,
Whole from his combat, to the royal court.
A space was soon made ready in the hall,
As the king ordered, for the voyagers.
    Then he who had come safely from the fight
Sat by the prince himself, kinsman by kinsman,
After the king in ceremonious words
Had welcomed heartily his loyal thane.
Next Hareth's daughter moved around the hall
With vessels full of mead – she loved the people –
And first of all she handed cups of wine

To the returning heroes. Hygelac
Began to question in a friendly way
His Geatish seafarers in the high hall,
And ask them how their enterprise had prospered.
He was consumed by curiosity:
'How did your journey go, dear Beowulf,
When you decided suddenly to sail
Far off and seek a fight in Heorot
Over the salt sea? Could you bring about
In any way a remedy to help
The great prince Hrothgar in his well known trouble?
I suffered great anxiety at heart, *
And, to speak truth, had little confidence
In the adventure of my dear retainer.
At length I pleaded with you not to go
To an encounter with that murderous sprite,
And prayed that you would let the Danes themselves
Make war on Grendel. I say thanks to God
That now again I see you safe and sound.'

   Beowulf spoke, the son of Edgetheow:
'Many men have now heard, lord Hygelac,
About our great encounter and the struggle
Between myself and Grendel in the place
Where he afflicted the heroic Danes
With many troubles and long-lasting hardships.
For all of that I took revenge, and now
No kin of Grendel anywhere on earth,
However long they live, immersed in sin,
Can boast again about his night-time raids.

   'I came up to the hall and greeted Hrothgar,
And straightaway the famous son of Halfdane,
As soon as he had heard what I proposed,

Assigned me to a seat by his own son.
The court was in good spirits; I have never
Seen in this world, under the vault of heaven,
Retainers at a finer festival.
Sometimes the glorious queen, the pledge of peace
Between the nations, went all round the hall,
In friendly fashion spoke to the young men,
Presenting some of them with precious rings
Before returning to her place at table.
And meanwhile Hrothgar's daughter, whom I heard
The people in the hall call Freawaru,
Was placing decorated cups of ale
Before the warriors of higher rank.
She has been promised, young and gold-adorned,
In marriage to the gracious son of Froda.
The Shilding lord, the keeper of the kingdom,
Has settled this, believing by this plan
That through this woman he can bring an end
To frequent strife and many deadly feuds.
But following a national defeat,
The deadly spear stays seldom long at rest,
However fair a foreign bride may be.
    'Then may the ruler of the Heathobards
And all the nation's thanes feel ill at ease
When in the hall he walks beside that maiden,
The noble Danish lady, with her band
Of courtiers, on whom are seen to shine
Heirlooms of ancestors adorned with rings,
The former treasures of the Heathobards
When they were the possessors of those weapons, . . .

XXVIIII–XXX

*Beowulf completes the digression and
reverts to the account of his fights.*

Until they put their lives at risk in war, *
Leading their dear companions to destruction.
An older spearman, while they sit at beer,
Remembering the slaughter of those men,
In spirit grim, will recognise some hilt
And, sad in heart, will start to tempt the mind
Of some young warrior by his recollections
And stir up violence, and speak these words:
"My friend, are you familiar with the sword,
The precious blade your father bore to battle,
Wearing his visor, on that last attack?
There the Danes slew him, and the powerful Shildings,
After the death of Withergild and the fall
Of many heroes, held the field of slaughter.
And now among those killers some young man
Struts in this hall triumphant in those trappings,
Boasts of the murder, bearing by his side
The precious sword which you by rights should own."
Thus he goes on, reminding and provoking
With bitter words, until the moment comes
That the princess's thane pays with his life
For what his father did; blood-soaked he lies
After the sword-blade's bite; the other thence
Escapes alive, he knows the country well.

Then on both sides the warriors' oaths are broken,
While Ingeld starts to harbour hostile feelings,
And in these seething sorrows starts to cool
His love towards his wife. I don't believe
The strong alliance and the pact of peace
Between the Heathobards and Danes will long
Remain intact. But now I will return
To speaking about Grendel, so that you,
Giver of rings, may clearly hear the tale
Of all that happened in our hand-encounter.

'After the gem of heaven had passed away
Beneath the ground, the angry guest arrived,
The hostile predator, to visit us
Where we, on guard, kept watch within the hall.
There Hondshoe in a murderous attack
Was fated to depart this life; at once
That well loved warrior lay slain by Grendel,
The fearsome monster killed him with his teeth,
And swiftly swallowed all his slaughtered corpse.
Nor was the bloody-fanged marauder, still
Intent on violence, planning yet to leave
The gold-hall empty-handed. Fierce and strong,
He tried me next, grabbed me with grasping hand.
A broad and wondrous bag hung down beside him,
Cunningly fastened, skilfully devised
By craft of devils, made of dragon's skin,
In which the wild attacker's purpose was
To carry me and many more away;
But it was not to be, for angrily
I stood upright. It is too long to tell
How I repaid that nation's ravager
For all the evil he had done to them.

There I, my prince, brought honour to your people.
He ran away, and for a little while
Continued to experience life's joys; *
However his right hand remained behind
In Heorot, whence wretchedly he fled
And sank down to the bottom of the lake.
    'The Shilding leader, for that bloody fight,
Richly rewarded me with plated gold
And many treasures, when the next day came
And we sat down together for a feast,
With songs and stories for our entertainment.
There the old king told tales of long ago,
Of which he knew full many, and at times
A nobleman melodiously plucked
The harp and sang a sad historic lay,
Which the great-hearted Shilding interspersed
With stirring talk of marvellous events;
Sometimes the white-haired warrior, bound by age,
Lamented his lost youth and battle-strength;
His breast within him seethed as, old in years,
He called to mind his many former deeds.
Thus in that hall the whole length of the day
We took our pleasures, till the next night came
Across mankind, and shortly after that
Came Grendel's mother, grieving for her harm,
Ready to wreak revenge, because her son
Had lost his life in battle with the Geats.
The monstrous woman there avenged her child,
Killing a warrior without remorse.
There the wise councillor called Ashhere
Departed from this life; nor could the Danes
When morning came cremate his corpse in flames

Or place their much loved comrade on a pyre.
Clutched in her arms she bore the body off,
Carried it to her home beneath the waters.
  'Of all the sorrows that had long beset
Hrothgar, the ruler of the people, that
Was the most grievous. Then the troubled prince
Implored me to attempt a valiant action
Amid the surging waters, and to risk
My life and win renown. He promised me
That he would well reward me for that deed.
Then, as is now well known, I went and found
The grim and grisly guardian of that pool.
There for a while was battle joined between us;
The water seethed with gore, and I cut off
The head of Grendel's mother in that hall
With a sharp sword. I came away alive
With difficulty – I was not yet doomed!
The prince of heroes then presented me,
The son of Halfdane, with a heap of treasures.

XXXI

*Beowulf presents his gifts from
Hrothgar to Hygelac and Hygd, and
Hygelac rewards him. Following the
death of Hygelac in battle and later
that of his son Heardred, Beowulf
becomes king and reigns until a
dragon attacks his people.*

'That honourable king fulfilled his promise,
According to the customs of the tribes,
And I was well rewarded for my strife;
I was presented by the son of Halfdane
With all the riches that I could desire.
These I now wish to bring and offer you,
Great warrior king, since I owe everything
To you alone; for I have few close kinsmen,
Apart from you, my uncle, Hygelac.'
   He bade them to bring in the boar-head banner,
The high-topped helmet and the shiny corslet
And ornate war-sword, and he spoke these words:
'This battle-gear the wise prince Hrothgar gave me,
But first of all he ordered me to tell you
Its noble history: King Heorogar,
The Shilding prince, owned it for many years,
Yet would not give the corslet to his son,
Brave Heoroweard, though he was dear to him.
Now, Hygelac, may you enjoy it well!'

I heard that after that four matching bay
Horses were brought into the hall, arrayed
In gorgeous trappings; he presented all
To Hygelac, the treasures and the horses.
So should a kinsman do, and not contrive
A web of malice around other kinsmen
By secret craft, or bring about the deaths
Of close companions; to his war-brave leader
Hygelac's nephew was entirely loyal,
And each was mindful of the other's good.
The necklace, as I heard, he gave to Hygd,
The wondrous jewel which Wealhtheow gave to him,
The prince's daughter, and three horses too,
Graceful and richly saddled; from that time
She always wore that jewel on her breast.

Thus Edgetheow's son, famous for warlike deeds,
Won honour by his virtuous behaviour.
He never slew his drunken hearth-companions.
Though a fierce fighter, he was mild in manner,
And the great gifts which God had granted him
He used, but only in a righteous cause.
Earlier in his life he was long held
In low repute among the Geats; the king
Gave him scant recognition in the mead-hall.
They rated him a slack and feeble prince;
But that all changed when, later on in life,
After these miseries he achieved great glory.

The warlike king ordered to be brought in
A gold-encrusted heirloom of King Hrethel.
Among the Geats there was no greater treasure
Than that fine sword; he laid it in the lap
Of Beowulf. With that he granted him

A hall, a princedom and seven thousand hides,
The power and privileges of that province
To be under the lordship of them both;
But Hygelac, being of higher rank,
Retained the final rule across that land.

Many years after this it came about,
When Hygelac had met his death in war,
And later still, when battle-swords had taken
The life of Heardred beneath the shield-wall,
When the fierce soldiers of the Swedish king
Had sought him out among the warring people
And viciously attacked Hygelac's heir,
That their broad kingdom passed into the hands
Of Beowulf; advanced in age and wise
He ruled it well for nigh on fifty years –
Till, suddenly, a dragon on dark nights
Began to take control. High on a heath
He kept a hoard inside a steep stone barrow.
Beside it lay an unfrequented path.
Some man or other passed thereby and went
Into the heathen hoard, and in his hands
Took a large cup, adorned with gold and jewels.
By no means did that dragon hide the fact
That while he was asleep he had been robbed
By a thief's cunning: those who lived nearby
Quickly discovered that he was enraged.

XXXII

A felon by chance finds a dragon's
hoard, and removes a precious vessel.
The hoard's origin is described. The
dragon discovers his loss.

The man who caused the dragon such distress
Did not on purpose break into the hoard,
But being destitute this nameless wretch
Was fleeing from the blows of punishment,
And, lacking shelter, pushed his way therein,
The guilty one. He soon became aware
That he was in dire peril from his host;
Swiftly therefore the hapless fugitive
Fled from that serpent, fearing his pursuit,
And bore away with him that precious vessel.
Within the cavern there were many more
Such ancient treasures, which an unknown man
Had carefully concealed there, all the heirlooms
And valued objects of some noble race.
Death took those men away in former times,
Leaving one lone survivor of the troop
To hold those riches, mourning for his friends,
Aware that he had very little time
To enjoy these ancient heirlooms. In the country
There stood a new-built barrow near the sea,
Close to the headland, difficult of access.
The guardian of the rings conveyed therein

Those noble treasures worthy to be stored,
The plated gold, and uttered a few words:
   'Earth, you must guard, now heroes cannot do so,
The warriors' possessions; for it was
From you that in past times men dug them up.
Now death in war and other deadly perils
Have taken all the members of my tribe;
From this world they have passed, and never more
Will know the joys of hall. No one remains
To wear the sword or clean the plated vessel,
The precious cup; the troop has all departed.
The warlike helmet will no longer hold
Its finely crafted gold; the cleaners sleep
Whose task was to prepare the battle-visor.
Likewise the chain-mail, which in battle used
To feel the bite of swords above the clash
Of shields, decays just like the warrior.
The pleasant music of the wood-framed harp
Is heard no more, nor does the graceful hawk
Swing swiftly through the hall, nor the fleet horse
Trample the pavement of the castle courtyard.'
   Thus sad in mind he spoke about his grief,
Living alone, when all the rest had gone;
Joyless he moved about by day and night,
Until death's fatal finger touched his heart.
An ancient predator, a cruel dragon,
Who flies about by night with fire encircled
Looking for barrows, found that precious treasure
Standing wide open. Dwellers in those parts
Soon learned to dread him; dragons by their nature
Have to seek out such heathen hoards of gold
Buried in earth, and guard them all their lives,

Although they benefit them not at all.
    So for three hundred years that mighty creature,
The people's foe, guarded the treasure-house
Beneath the ground, until one single man
Enraged his spirit. He took the plated cup,
Offered it as a peace pledge to his lord,
And thus the buried treasure was disturbed
And partly looted, and that wretched man
Was granted what he asked for, while his lord
Looked on that work of ancient craftsmanship
Unseen before for many generations.
    The serpent then woke up, and strife returned;
The fearsome creature looked around the stone
And found the footprints of his enemy,
Who in that furtive enterprise had stepped
So close beside the sleeping dragon's head.
An undoomed man can sometimes be preserved
If luck and the Lord's grace are on his side!
The guardian of the hoard sought frenziedly
Around that place, wanting to find the man
Who had so sorely harmed him while he slept.
Hot and enraged he searched all round the mound
On the outside, but no man could he find
In that waste place; his thoughts began to turn
To battle and a violent revenge.
He went a few more times inside the barrow
To seek the cup, but soon he knew for sure
That someone had indeed purloined that gold
And noble treasure. Angrily he waited
Till evening came. The keeper of the treasure
Planned to take payment for his precious cup
Through hostile flames. The day came to an end

As he desired. He would no longer linger
Beside the wall, but set off, armed with fire.
The onset of that feud was truly fearsome
For dwellers in that land, just as its end
Was sudden and disastrous for their ruler.

XXXIII

*Homes of the Geats, including
Beowulf's, are destroyed by the
dragon. Beowulf's part in the battle in
which Hygelac died is described, as is
his refusal to rule instead of Heardred
until the latter's death.*

The dragon then began to spew out flames
And set alight their houses and their homesteads.
The blazing fires brought terror to the people;
The flying raider did not mean to leave
Anything living. Everyone could see
The dragon's depredations far and wide,
And how that enemy oppressed and harassed
The Geatish folk. Before the break of day
He shot back to his hoard, his secret cavern,
Where he felt safe within the rock-girt barrow,
Trusting in that and in his warlike skills;
But in the end that faith would prove unfounded.
   News of the terror was at once conveyed
To Beowulf, including that his home,
The regal house from which he ruled the Geats,
Had been demolished in those sweeping fires.
To that good man it was the greatest sorrow,
Grief in his heart. It seemed to the wise king
That he must have provoked the eternal Lord
To bitter anger by some grave offence

Against the ancient law. His breast was filled
With dark despair, unlike his usual mood.
  The fiery dragon with his flaming breath
Had utterly destroyed the nation's stronghold
Beside the sea. For this the warrior king,
The Geatish prince, prepared to take revenge.
He ordered to be made a special shield
Entirely out of iron, because he knew
That wood could not protect him against fire.
The transient lifetime of that best of princes
Here in this world was moving to its end,
And numbered also were the dragon's days,
Although it had long held the treasure hoard.
The lord of rings disdained that he should gather
An army to confront that flying menace.
He did not fear to take him on himself,
Nor did he highly rate the dragon's skill
And power in battle. Many times before
He had survived some perilous encounter
On which he had embarked, some clash of battle
After, victorious, he had cleansed the hall
Of Hrothgar, when he fought and crushed to death
The Grendel family, that hateful kindred.
  Among those fierce encounters not the least
Was that in which King Hygelac was slain,
The gracious ruler of the Geatish people,
The son of Hrethel, in the brutal battle
In Frisia. He died from loss of blood,
Struck down by swords. Thence Beowulf escaped
By his own skill – he swam away by sea,
Carrying with him thirty suits of armour.
The people of the Hetware who had borne

Their battle-shields against him had no cause
To triumph in their fighting skills, for few
Of those who came to war went home again.
    The son of Edgetheow, wretched and alone,
Swam back across the ocean to his country.
Queen Hygd then offered Beowulf the kingdom,
Care of its hoard and treasures and the throne.
She feared her young son would not have the power
To hold the realm against marauding foes
Now that his father Hygelac was dead.
In spite of that he steadfastly refused
To become ruler over Heardred,
The luckless prince, or let himself be king;
But he became a wise adviser to him,
Giving him friendly guidance, till the time
That he could fully take upon himself
To rule the kingdom of the Geatish nation.
    One day some exiled men came to his court *
Over the lake, the sons of Ohthere; †
They had rebelled against their Shilfing lord,
The famous prince and greatest of sea-kings,
Treasure-dispenser in the realm of Sweden;
But through that hospitality the son
Of Hygelac met his untimely end,
Mortally wounded by the strokes of swords.
And after Heardred's death the Swedish king,
Onela son of Ongentheow went home,
Allowing Beowulf to hold the throne
And rule the Geats; and he was a good king.

XXXIIII

*Beowulf sets out with a troop to
confront the dragon. He recounts
major events in the family of Hygelac,
in the course of which he describes
the grief of a theoretical father
whose son has been hanged.*

He thought to take revenge in later days
For his lord's death, and aided Eadgils
In his distress, supporting Ohthere's son
Across the frozen lake with men and weapons. *
Eadgils there repaid the Swedish king
For his cold cares, depriving him of life.
    Thus Edgetheow's son had come away unscathed
From every fight and dangerous encounter,
Until the day came when he was to meet
The dragon; he set out in mighty wrath,
The Geatish leader, with eleven men,
To seek the serpent out. He had been told
How this campaign of hatred had begun,
This malice towards men. The precious cup
Had come into his hands, brought by the thief
Who found it; he became the thirteenth man
Among that troop, a heavy-hearted captive,
Who was compelled to guide them to the place.
Against his will he led them to the mound,
The cavern under ground, close to the sea,

Full of rich ornaments and works of art,
Whose whereabouts was known to him alone.
The fierce and ancient guardian had held
Those treasures in the earth for many years,
Jewels and gold and rings. It was no place
For one averse to risk to enter in.
The battle-hardened king sat on the headland,
The Geatish prince, and to his hearth-companions
He uttered words of comfort, but his heart
Was sad and restless, keen for mortal combat.
The fate was all too near that would assail
The agèd warrior, seek out his soul,
Separate life from body; not much longer
Would flesh enclose the spirit of the prince.
    Beowulf spoke, the son of Edgetheow:
'As a young man I came through many battles
And times of peril, as I well recall.
When I was seven years old the ring-giver,
The country's leader, took me from my father,
King Hrethel sheltered me and brought me up,
Invited me to feasts and gave me treasure,
For he was always mindful of our kinship;
And in that life as warrior in his courts
I was as close to him as his own sons,
Herebald, Hathkin and my Hygelac.
The eldest suffered an untimely death
Unfittingly, when the fraternal hand
Of Hathkin shot his kinsman with an arrow
From his horn-bow; he took aim at the mark,
But missed; the missile struck and killed his brother.
That sinful deed could not be expiated
By money payment, though it caused great heartbreak.

The prince was slain, his death went unavenged.
   'In the same way it would be sorrowful
For an old man to live to see his son
Ride on the gallows; then he will lament
And sing a song of sadness, while his heir
Is hanging as a comfort to the ravens.
Advanced in years, he can do nothing for him,
Come to his aid. He will recall each morning
The parting of his son; he will not wish
To await another heir within his dwelling
When this one has, by a distressing death,
Paid for his deeds. Sad-hearted he will see
In his son's house the wine-hall bare and empty,
Home to the winds; the joys are all departed,
No warriors, no horsemen come and go,
No more is heard the music of the harp
Or entertainment, as there was before.

XXXV

*Beowulf continues with an account of
the wars between Geats and Swedes,
and mentions his part in the battle in
Frisia in which Hygelac died.
He approaches the dragon and the
fight begins. His accompanying
warriors flee to the woods.*

'He goes then to his chamber all alone
And mourns his missing son; his home and lands
Now seem too spacious for his lonely needs.
Just so the ruler of the Geatish people
Suffered the surging sorrow in his heart
For Herebald his son; but he could not
Impose due retribution on the slayer,
Nor punish him with hostile penalties,
Although the killer was not dear to him;
And through that grief which painfully beset him
He gave up all the pleasures of mankind
And chose God's light; he left to his descendants *
His country and the nation's capital,
As a good king should, when he left this life.
    'Fierce strife and warfare then arose between †
The Swedes and Geats across the waterways
After the death of Hrethel. The bold sons
Of Ongentheow had no wish for peace
Across the sea, but around Hresnaberg ‡

They often undertook ferocious raids.
As is well known my kinsmen sought revenge
For these attacks and crimes, though one of them
Paid for it with his life, a heavy price;
Hathkin the Geatish king died in that war.
Next day, I heard, his brother Hygelac
Had vengeance on his slayer by the sword
When Ongentheow encountered Eofor;
His helmet split in two; the agèd Shilfing *
Fell lifeless; Eofor had not restrained
His hand in issuing that fatal blow.

   'In later life I too contrived to pay,
With my sharp sword in war, for all the treasures
That Hygelac my lord had granted me,
And the possession of a fine demesne.
With me at hand he had no need to seek
Fighters from Gepids, Danes and other tribes,
Or pay with gold for Swedish mercenaries.
Always in battle I was at the front
Leading his troops; and so I will go on
As long as I have life, and while this sword
Lasts, which has served me in all kinds of trouble,
Since in the battle I slew Dagraven, †
The Frankish champion and standard-bearer.
That famous warrior did not live to carry
Armour and loot back to the Frisian king,
But died in battle; it was not my blade
That broke his body, but a wrestling grip
Ended his heartbeats. Now my hand shall use
The sword's sharp edge in fighting for the hoard.

   'I survived many battles in my youth,
And now again, old guardian of the people,

I will join fight, attempting to do deeds
Worthy of honour, if this evil-doer
Emerges from his cavern and attacks.'
    He greeted then each of the warriors,
Brave helmet-wearers, for the final time,   *
His dear companions: 'I would not bear blade
Or sword against the serpent if I knew
How otherwise to grapple with the monster,
As formerly I used my grip on Grendel.
But now I can expect hot hostile flame,
Poisonous breath, and so I have upon me
My shield and corslet. I will not retreat
A foot's length from the keeper of the barrow;
And it shall go for us two at the wall
As fate, the ruler of mankind, decides.
My heart is ready; I will say no more
About my chances with the flying foe.
Wearing your chain-mail and your battle-armour
Wait on this mound, until it can be seen
Which one of us can best survive the wounds
Exchanged between us in this mortal conflict.
This fight is not for you, nor is it right
For any other man except myself
To pit his strength against this monstrous beast,
Take on the challenge. By my courage I
Shall either win the gold or lose the fight,   †
When deadly strife would take away your lord.'
    Then the brave hero rose up with his shield,
Strong in his helmet, bore his coat of mail
Under the stony cliff; he trusted in
Himself alone; that's not the coward's way!
He who had lived through many a clash of arms

Saw that an arch of stone stood by the wall,
And there a stream of blazing flame burst out
From underneath the barrow, so that he
Could not endure the heat for any while
Close to the hoard. The ruler of the Geats,
Enraged, let out a roar; this call to battle
Resounded loudly under the grey stone.
Hatred was roused; the guardian of the treasure
Instantly recognised a human voice;
The time had long since passed to sue for peace!
    First came the monster's flaming poisonous breath
Out from the cavern, with a sound like thunder.
Beside the mound the leader of the Geats
Swung round his shield towards his gruesome foe,
And the coiled creature braced himself for combat.
The warrior-king had drawn his sword already,
The ancient heirloom with its sharp, bright blade.
Neither of those antagonists was free
From fear, as they confronted one another.
Still steadfast stood the leader of that troop
With his tall shield, and waited in his armour.
The blazing serpent tightly coiled himself,
Then bounded forward hastening to his fate.
His shield protected well the life and body
Of the great prince, but for a shorter while
Than he had hoped, since fate for the first time
Did not allow him triumph in a fight,
Success in strife. The ruler of the Geats
Raised up his arm and struck the gaudy monster
Hard with his shining sword, and its sharp edge
Bit, but not far enough, into his bone,
Just when the people's king, in dire distress,

Had need of it. Then was the barrow's keeper
Angry in heart after that battle-wound,
And spewed out deadly fire; the hostile flames
Spread widely, and the leader of the Geats
Was in no case to claim a victory.
His famous sword had failed him in the fight,
That fine old steel, as it should not have done.

It was no easy journey that the great
Kinsman of Edgetheow soon would have to make,
Leaving this world. He must, against his will,
Take up his dwelling in another place.
Thus every man must leave these transient days.

After a pause the fighters clashed again;
The dragon's heart was boosted, and his breath
Renewed within his breast. The prince meanwhile
Found himself closely hemmed in by the flames.
His close companions, sons of noblemen,
Did not approach and join him in his need,
But, lacking valour, fled into the woods
To save their lives; just one of them remained,
Whose heart was overcome with grief and sorrow.
For a right-minded warrior the ties
Of kinsmanship can never be denied.

XXXVI

*Wiglaf is introduced, and makes a
speech urging that the retainers should
go to Beowulf's aid. He goes alone,
but Beowulf is severely wounded.*

His name was Wiglaf, son of Weohstan,
Alfhere's cousin, from the Shilfing clan,
A well loved shield-bearer; he saw his lord
Under his visor struggling in the heat.
He thought of all the favours that the prince
Had granted him, and of the wealthy home
And other honours of the Wagmundings,
With the distinguished status of his father.
He could not then hold back, but grabbed his shield,
His yellow targe, and drew his ancient sword,
Which Eanmund, son of Ohthere, had owned,
Who as a lordless exile met his death
By Weohstan's hand. He took back to his lord *
And kinsman Onela as battle-booty
This sword, the work of giants in olden times,
Together with his bright-ringed coat of mail
And gleaming helmet; Onela gave back
To Weohstan the armour of his nephew;
The king did not make mention that the victim
Of this encounter was his brother's son.
He kept that ornate shield and sword and corslet
For many years, until his son attained

The rank of warrior, like his ancestors;
Then he passed all that armour on to Wiglaf,
While he, being old, departed from this life.
It was the first time that this young retainer
Had to take part in fight beside his lord.
His spirit did not melt, nor did the sword
Bequeathed him by his father fade away
In battle, as the serpent soon discovered.

    Wiglaf, consumed by grief, then made a speech,
Addressed his comrades with some noble words:
'I call to mind the time when we drank mead
And made a promise to our generous lord
That, when the need arose, as now it does,
We would repay him for our battle-gear,
Our helmets and hard swords. Therefore he chose
Us from his army for this enterprise,
Gave us this honour and awarded treasures,
Because he judged us worthy helmet-wearers
And brave spear-fighters, though our lord proposed
To undertake this valiant deed alone,
Since, more than any other man alive,
He has fulfilled the greatest feats of glory.
Now has the day arrived when our dear chief
Requires the aid of active warriors.
Let us go to him while this fearsome heat
Persists, the awful terror of the flames.
God knows that I would much prefer to let
The fire wrap round my body by my lord.
It seems to me not right that we should take
Our shields back home, unless we first have slain
The foe, and saved our Geatish leader's life.
I know for sure that he has not deserved

To undertake alone the pain and danger
For all the Geats, and perish in the strife.
So let our swords and helmets, shields and corslets
Be joined with his in challenging the dragon.'
    He then advanced across the noisome fumes
To his lord's aid, and uttered a few words:
'Dear Beowulf, you are fulfilling still
The honourable pledges that you made
Long since in time of youth, you will not let
Your glory weaken while you are alive.
Resolute prince, while now, brave in your deeds,
You strive to save your life with all your strength
Against this mighty foe, I will support you.'
    The angry serpent, the ferocious creature,
Launched an attack now for the second time,
Belching out flames against his enemies,
The hated humankind. The rounded shield
Of the young warrior was consumed by fire,
His corslet could not give him any help,
So he was straight away compelled to seek
Safety behind his kinsman's shield, his own
Being rendered useless. Then the warrior king
Braced himself up and struck a mighty blow,
So that his sword stuck in the dragon's head,
Thrust with great force; but Nailing broke apart,
Beowulf's ancient and grey-coated sword
Failed in the fight; it was not granted him
That the sword's edge could help him in that battle.
His hand was, I have heard, too powerful,
And often struck blows with far greater force
Than any sword, however strong, could take,
Which worked to his advantage not at all.

For the third time the spoiler of the people,
The fierce fire-dragon, hot and fighting-ready,
Rushed at the brave man as he backed away,
And tightly seized his throat with his sharp tusks,
So that the hero's blood poured out in waves.

XXXVII

*The dragon is killed, but Beowulf's
wound festers, and he asks Wiglaf to
enter the hoard and bring out some
of the treasure for him to see.*

Then, at his monarch's need, as I heard tell,
The bold retainer showed his lasting valour
And skill and firm resolve, as was his nature.
He went not for the head, but still his hand
Was burnt while running to his kinsman's aid;
The well-armed warrior struck the vicious stranger
A little lower down, so that his sword,
Ornate and plated, sank into the dragon,
And thereupon the fire began to fail.
The king himself recovered then his senses,
And, drawing the sharp dagger that he carried
Upon his corslet, started to cut through
The middle of the serpent. Both together
They felled the fiend, their valour took his life,
And the two noble kinsmen there destroyed him.
Thus should an honourable thane behave
In time of need. But for the prince it was
The final act of triumph in the world
Achieved by his own deeds. And now the wound
Which the earth-dragon gave him had begun
To swell and fester; he became aware
The poison was at work within his breast

With horrible effects. The wise chief then
Went and sat on a seat beside the wall.
He gazed upon this ruined work of giants,
Saw how the earth-hall stood within stone arches
Firm on their pillars, while his matchless thane
Washed with his hands the battle-bloodied prince
And rinsed his lord with water, as he sat
Exhausted from the fight, and loosed his helmet.

    Beowulf made a speech, despite his wound,
His deadly injury; he knew full well
That his life's span was coming to its end,
His earthly pleasures, that his count of days
Was over now, and death extremely near:
'Now I would give my war-gear to my son,
Had any heir been granted to my body
To follow after me. I ruled this nation
For fifty years. There was no people's king
Among the neighbouring tribes who dared attack me,
Or threaten me with military might.
I stayed at home for my allotted span
As ruler, and looked after my own people,
Joined no conspiracies in foreign lands,
Nor compromised myself with unjust oaths.
For all this I am able to rejoice,
Despite my mortal wounds, nor will the King
Of Men have cause to blame me for the murder
Of kinsmen, when my body leaves this life.

    'Go forth now quickly, my beloved Wiglaf,
To see the hoard beneath these old grey stones,
Now that the dragon, slain by grievous wounds,
Lies dead, shorn of his treasure. Hurry, so
That I may view this trove of ancient wealth,

Look on the golden ornaments, and gaze
Upon the bright and sparkling gems; then I
Can the more easily give up my life,
With the high office I so long have held.'

XXXVIII

*Wiglaf brings out treasures and
attends to Beowulf, who gives
instructions for his funeral and dies.*

The son of Weohstan instantly obeyed
The urgent bidding of his wounded lord,
And in his armour and his corslet strode
Into the barrow. The victorious thane
Saw there in front of him a mass of treasure,
With golden vessels glinting on the ground
And wondrous objects hanging from the walls
Around the den of the dusk-flying dragon,
And cups and goblets of that ancient clan,
Which, lacking those who should have cared for them,
Lay battered and unpolished on the floor.
There too were many old and rusty helmets,
And bracelets fashioned with consummate skill.
(Possession of a hoard of gold and treasure *
Can easily provoke excessive pride
In any man, though he may try to hide it.)
    Wiglaf saw too a standard made of gold
Suspended high above the hoard, the best
Of banners, by the finest craftsmen's hands.
From this shone out a light, so that he could
Survey the ground and look on all these marvels.
No dragon threatened now, for the sword's blade
Had taken him away. Then I heard tell

That Wiglaf robbed that hoard within the barrow,
The ancient work of giants, and in his grasp
He loaded himself up with cups and dishes,
As many as he could; he also took
The gleaming banner, brightest of all beacons.
The old king's steel-edged sword had put to rest
The guardian who so long had kept that treasure,
And in the middle of the night had waged
War with hot flaming fire outside the hoard
Until he met his death. The brave retainer
Was in a hurry to get back again,
Anxious to find out if the Geatish prince,
Whom he had left behind so sorely sick,
Was still alive, and, carrying the treasures,
He found his famous lord where he had left him,
Bleeding and moving towards his end of life.
He sprinkled him with water once again,
Until he managed to bring out some words.
The warrior-king, the old man in his grief,
Gazed at the gold, and finally he spoke:
    'I say thanks to the Lord, the King of Glory,
Eternal God, for all these precious things
Which I here look on, that I have been granted
To win them for my folk before I die.
And now that I have sold my agèd life
For this great hoard of treasure, Wiglaf, you
Must be the next protector of my people
In all their needs, for I may stay no longer.
Command the heroes after my cremation,
To build a barrow up above the shore,
High on the headland which is called Hronsness, *
As a memorial for my tribe, and sailors

Shall call it Beowulf's Barrow, men who drive
Great ships afar over the surging sea.'
   He then took from his neck a golden collar,
The valiant prince, and passed it to his thane;
To the young warrior he gave that necklet
With his chain-mail and finely crafted helmet,
And bade him use them well. He spoke again:
'You are the last survivor of our kindred,
The Wagmundings, for fate has swept away
Our other kinsmen at their destined hours,
Those gallant men, and I must follow them.'
   These were his last words, uttered from the heart
Of the old man, before he chose the pyre,
Fiery cremation, and his soul went forth
Out of his breast to seek the righteous judgement.

XXXVIIII

*The warriors who had fled shamefully
emerge from the woods, and
are rebuked by Wiglaf.*

Great grief was that to the young warrior
When on the ground he saw his dearest lord,
Alive no more. The slayer likewise lay,
The awesome earth-dragon, deprived of life,
Cut down in fight. No longer could the serpent
With twisted coils control its hoard of rings,
For the blade's edge, well hammered by the smith,
Hardened in combat, had removed him hence,
So the wide-flier, grounded by his wounds,
Fell to the earth beside his treasure-store.
Never again across the midnight sky
Would he go flying and display himself,
Proud in his wealth; but he lay on that land,
Slain by the skilful handwork of the hero.
Few men have come out best, as I have heard,
However bold and mighty they might be,
From combat with a foe with poisonous breath,
Or setting foot within a treasure-chamber
If they have found its guardian awake
And watchful in the barrow. Beowulf
Paid with his life for winning of that gold;
Each of the combatants had reached the end
Predestined in this transitory life.

Not long thereafter those who had held back
From fighting left the woods, the weak oath-breakers,
Ten men in all, who had not dared before
To use their spears in their lord's pressing need.
Shamefaced they bore their shields and battle-gear
To where the old man lay. They looked on Wiglaf,
Who sat worn out beside his lord and tried
To wake him up with water, but in vain.
Try as he might, he could not bring him back
To life and overturn the will of God,
Whose rule and judgement governed every man
In every way then as they do today.
    The young man had no difficulty finding
Grim words for those who had abandoned valour.
Wiglaf the son of Weohstan spoke these words,
He looked with heavy heart on those he scorned:
'He who would speak the truth can justly say
Of the great prince who gave you all the treasures
And battle-gear that you are wearing now,
When on the mead-benches he often gave
Helmets and corslets to his hall-retainers,
The best that far and wide he could obtain,
That wretchedly he wasted all that armour,
As can be seen, when battle came upon him.
The conduct of his chosen warriors
Conferred no credit on our country's king;
However, God, the Lord of victories,
Granted that he should win revenge alone
For his own death by wielding of his sword,
While I was able to give little aid
In my attempt to join him in the strife;
But I at least tried to support my kinsman,

Although it proved to be beyond my powers.
Yet when I struck the slayer with my sword
It always weakened him, so that the fire
Shot out less fiercely from his head. Too few
Defenders came and thronged about their prince
When need arose. Now shall the gifts of treasure
And swords, all your hereditary rights
To lands and homesteads be forever lost
To you and all your kin, all hopes and joys,
When far and wide the nobles learn about
Your flight and your dishonourable deed.
For every warrior in every land
Death would be better than a life of shame.'

XL

*A messenger reports back to the main
body of the Geats, forecasting their
future disaster at the hands of enemies,
and recounting the previous history of
the Geatish/Swedish wars.*

He ordered that the outcome of the fight
Should be reported up above the cliff,
At the enclosure where the troop of nobles
Had sat throughout the morning, sad at heart,
And hoping that their dear prince would return,
But fearing it might be his final day.
Up to the headland rode the messenger
And made a full announcement to those men
Of all that happened at the dragon's den:
'Now is the leader of the Geatish nation,
The source of all our hopes, consigned to death,
Slain by the onslaught of the vicious serpent.
The body of his deadly enemy
Lies lifeless on the ground beside him, felled
By dagger-thrusts, for Beowulf with his sword
Had failed in any way to wound the monster.
Wiglaf, the son of Weohstan, sits beside him,
Brave warrior beside his leader's corpse,
With weary spirit guards both friend and foe.
    'Now can our land expect a time of war,
When the king's death becomes known far and wide

Among the Franks and Frisians. Deadly strife
Arose between us and the Frankish realms
When Hygelac went raiding with a fleet
In Frisian lands. The Hetware beat him there
Because they could deploy a larger force,
So that his troop was destined for defeat,
And he too died among his foot-soldiers.
He won no victor's booty for his men,
And since that time the Merovingian kings
Have always looked upon us with disfavour.
    'Nor have I any better expectation
Of peace and good will from our Swedish neighbours,
But it is widely known that Ongentheow *
Ended the life of Hathkin son of Hrethel
Near Ravenswood, after the Geatish army
Had rashly raided into Shilfing land;
Then the old fierce and battle-hardened Swede
Counter-attacked and killed the sailor king
And rescued from captivity his wife,
Mother of Ohthere and Onela,
And, having done that, chased his enemies
Until they scarcely had the strength to flee
To Ravenswood, their leader being lost.
He then surrounded with his larger force
Those wearied with their wounds, who had survived
The earlier fight, and threatened all night long
Annihilation of that wretched band,
And said that in the morning he would slay
Most of them with the edges of the sword,
And hang the others on the gallows-tree
For the enjoyment of the carrion-birds.
    'But with the dawn relief and comfort came

To those in desperate plight, soon as they heard
The horns and trumpet-calls of Hygelac's men,
When their great leader with his trusted troops
Came following up the route that they had taken.

XLI

Death of Ongentheow.
The Geats go to view the
dragon's corpse and the hoard.

'The bloody signs of conflict and of carnage
Between the Swedes and Geats spread far and wide,
As the two armies clashed with one another.
But in the end the famous Ongentheow,
The fierce old fighter with his closest comrades,
Was forced in his distress to turn away
From battle and seek safety in his stronghold.
He knew about the military skill
Of Hygelac, his prowess in the field,
And feared that his own power was not enough
To hold him off and to resist the seamen
And to protect his hoard and wife and children,
So he retired to his defensive wall.
The Geats pursued the fleeing Swedish troops,
Hygelac's banners passed across the outworks,
And his men thronged up to the boundary.
There white-haired Ongentheow was forced to stop
And had to yield to Eofor's demand
To fight him and his brother, the two sons
Of Wonred. Wulf then struck him with his weapon,
So that the blood from underneath his hair
Poured down his face. The agèd Shilfing was
Not yet dismayed, but he at once repaid

That savage sword-stroke with a worse one back,
And, speedy as he was, the son of Wonred
Could not return the agèd warrior's blow.
For Ongentheow, that old and doughty chief,
Had cut right through his helmet to his head;
The blood poured from him, and he fell to earth.
He was not dead, but in due time recovered,
Although the wound had done him lasting harm.
Then Eofor, brave thane of Hygelac,
Seeing his brother lying on the ground,
Reached with his sword across the guarding shield,
His ancient, giant-made sword, and smote the king
Hard on his helmet, so that Ongentheow,
The country's guardian, fell, bereft of life.
    'As soon as they controlled the battlefield,
Many men came and bound up Eofor's brother
And quickly lifted him and bore him off,
While Eofor despoiled the fallen king,
Removed his iron corslet and his sword
And helmet, and conveyed the old man's armour
To Hygelac, who graciously received
Those trappings, making promise of reward,
Which duly he performed in sight of all.
The son of Hrethel, leader of the Geats,
When he came home repaid those battle-feats
Of both the brothers with exceeding treasure,
And gave them each a hundred thousand units *
Of land, as well as copious twisted rings.
No one could blame him for rewarding them
So richly for such brave and glorious deeds;
And also, as a further mark of favour
He gave his only daughter's hand in marriage

To Eofor, a blessing for his home.
   'This is the ancient feud and deadly hatred
Which brings me to expect the Swedish people
Will make war on us when they hear our lord
Is lifeless, he who previously held
Kingdom and hoard against our enemies, *
Ruled for our nation's good, and furthermore
Did many deeds of bravery and valour.
Now we should hasten to our ring-giver,
The nation's king, and bring him to his pyre.
And when the time comes to cremate the hero,
There shall not melt with him only a part
Of this great hoard of treasures, numberless
Jewels and golden objects, grimly won
And purchased at the cost of his own life;
The flames shall eat them all, the fire consume them, †
No warrior shall wear them for remembrance,
Nor fair maid sport these rings about her neck,
But, sad in heart, deprived of such adornments,
Long shall they tread the bitter paths of exile,
Now that their battle-lord has passed away
From sport and laughter and all other joys.
So, in the cold of dawn shall many a spear
Be raised up in the hands of fighting men,
The music of the harp will not be heard
To rouse men from their sleep, but the dark raven
Shall call out many times over doomed men,
Telling the eagle that he has fed well
While he has shared his carrion with the wolf.'
   In such terms did this warrior end his message
Of woe, and time would tell he did not lie.
The troop rose up and grieving they set off

With gushing tears from under Eagle's Ness
To view this wondrous spectacle. They found
Lifeless and lying on his bed of rest
The one who gave them rings in former times.
The famous hero's final day had come;
The warlike king, the ruler of the Geats,
Had died a death for men to marvel at.
Beside him on the field they saw the serpent,
That wondrous loathsome creature, whose own flames
Had scorched and burnt its multi-coloured corpse.
Stretched out it measured fifty feet in length.
Until then he had known the joys of flying
During dark nights, and then he had come down
By day to occupy his secret den;
Now he was fast in death, and never more
Would seek the comfort of his earthen cave.
Beside him scattered on the ground there lay
Flagons and cups and dishes; precious swords
Were eaten through with rust, as they had lain
In the earth buried for a thousand years,
That huge and rich inheritance of wealth,
The gold of ancient men, bound by a spell
By which no man would be allowed to enter
The treasure-cavern, unless God himself,
The King of victories, mankind's protector,
Should grant it to whichever man he pleased,
As he thought fit, to open up that hoard.

XLII

*Wiglaf instructs the Geats to transport
Beowulf's body and the treasures
to the funeral place.*

So it was plain that he who wrongly stored
Those precious artefacts beneath the wall
Produced no happy outcome for himself.
The dragon sought revenge by slaying Geats,
And now the feud was angrily repaid.
No one can know for certain when a man,
However brave, will reach his final day,
When he no longer with his friends and kinsmen
Can sojourn in the mead-hall. So it was
With Beowulf when he took on the fight
Against the fierce custodian of the barrow.
He knew not how his death would come about.
(The mighty prince who placed the treasure there
Had put a spell upon it which would last
Until the Day of Doom, that any man
Who robbed that place should be condemned of sin,
Confined to hell in grievous punishment.
But Beowulf had gone there not for gold, *
First having sought the favour of the Lord.)
   Wiglaf the son of Weohstan spoke to them:
'Often the actions of one man can bring
Affliction and distress to many others,
And so it is with us. Hard as we tried,

We were unable to dissuade our prince,
Our much loved lord, by any argument,
From an encounter with the treasure-keeper,
Bidding him let him lie where he so long
Had lived, continue in his dwelling place
Until the world should end. But he maintained
His high ideals. The hoard so sadly won
Can now be seen; that venture was too hard
Which our brave king was drawn to undertake.
I have been in and looked upon it all
When I was able to, though not invited
To enter as a welcome visitor.
I quickly grabbed an armful of the treasure
And brought it here outside to show my king;
He was still then alive, aware and conscious.
The old man in his grief said many things,
Bade me to greet you kindly, and requested
That you would build a tall and mighty barrow
To stand as a memorial of his deeds
Upon the spot where first his pyre has stood.
He was the worthiest of warriors
In this wide world as long as he had life
And could take comfort from the wealth and safety
That in his reign his countrymen enjoyed.
Let us make haste and go together now
To see this store of finely crafted gems
Inside the cavern. I will lead you there,
So that you can inspect from close at hand
The rings and gleaming gold. Make the bier ready
Forthwith, so that when we come back to you
We can at once convey the lord we loved
Into the place where he must long remain

Under the guardianship of the Almighty.'
    The son of Weohstan, the courageous hero,
Gave orders then to all the warriors
Who owned estates and companies of men
That they should gather wood from far away
And build a worthy pyre for their great king.
'Now must the fire, the towering smoky flame,
Consume the foremost of our fighting men,
Who often held the field when showers of iron
And storms of arrows urged from well-strung bows
Whirred past the shield-wall, and the feathered shaft
Propelled the sharp point to its fateful goal.'
    Wiglaf then called together seven thanes
From the king's special company, the best
Retainers, and himself, as one of eight,
Entered the home of their late enemy;
One of them went ahead, bearing a torch.
Seeing those treasures lying on the ground
Unguarded and abandoned in the hall,
They did not hesitate to grab it up,
And as they bore it rapidly away
They little mourned its previous possessor,
But cast the dragon down into the sea
Over the precipice, and let the waves
Take off the former keeper of the hoard.
The countless pieces of rich twisted gold
Were loaded onto wagons, and the prince,
The old and noble warrior was borne
To the high headland looking out to sea.

XLIII

A pyre is prepared, a mound raised,
and the treasures buried.
The funeral takes place.

The Geatish people then prepared a pyre
Firm on the earth, and hung around with helmets
And shields and corslets, just as he had asked,
And in the middle mourning warriors
Laid down their mighty prince, their much loved lord.
The grief-struck Geats raised up a funeral pyre
On the high cliff, the biggest ever yet;
The wood-smoke rose up dark above the flames
And the fire roared, mixed with the sound of weeping,
Till at its core the heat consumed the bones.
With grieving hearts and minds they mourned their
    lord,
While an old woman with her hair bound up
Sad and with sorrow sang a lamentation
For Beowulf, foretelling that she feared
Days of great hardship, many massacres,
Horrors of war, shame and captivity.
Heaven received the smoke, and there the Geats
Erected on the cliff a broad high mound
Which seafarers could see from far away.
They made the beacon for that mighty king
In just ten days, and built a wall around it
There where the fire had been, made it as well

As those who were most skilful could contrive it.
Into that barrow they placed all the rings
And jewels and other trappings which the men
Had previously taken from the hoard;
They put those treasures back into the earth,
Gold in the dust, where it now still remains,
Useless to men as it has always been.

Brave warriors then rode around the barrow,
The sons of princes, twelve of them in all,
Wishing to mourn their king, bewail their grief,
Put into speech their feelings for their hero.
They praised his virtues and nobility
And deeds of valour, as it is most fitting
That men should praise their generous lord in words
And love him in their hearts when the time comes
For his great soul to leave his human body.
They said that of the kings in all the world
He was the mildest and most generous,
Most kind to all his people and in all
His life most eager to have lived with honour.

Notes

In these notes the line numbers of the original Old English are given in brackets.

p. 3* (62), 'I heard': The poet frequently inserts such statements implying that he is reporting a story he has himself heard from someone else.

p. 3† (62): Owing to a serious scribal error at this point something is missing, including the name of this daughter; even the name of Onela is reconstructed and uncertain.

p. 4* (82–5): As indeed would in due course happen, apparently in reprisals following the failed attempt to settle hostilities with the Heathobards by the marriage of Freawaru and Ingeld; see p. 87.

p. 6* (123), 'thirty': This number is several times used to represent exaggerated scale.

p. 7* (168–9): The interpretation of these lines is problematical, as notes in any of the editions will reveal. It seems to mean that by some divine edict Hrothgar's throne was immune from the attacks; we later learn of similar magical protections of individuals, such as of Grendel from swords on p. 34.

p. 8* (175–88): The general tenor of the poem anachronistically implies that its world is Christian (though there are no references to anything relating to the New Testament), and this passage has the Danes reverting to pre-Christian practices in their despair.

p. 19* (455): Weyland was a master smith in Germanic mythology to whom various stories are attached. The best weapons are often attributed to him.

p. 20* (478–9): Occasional throwaway references to God, sometimes apparently at variance with the action of the poem, seem more likely to be conventional insertions rather than hinting at some complex theological implication. They raise the question of whether the poem as it stands represents a fairly accurate version of its 'original' composition, or whether it has been subjected to minor modifications during the course of transmission, in cases like this by a Christian interpolator. If so, he would have had to take some trouble, since, as in this case, they fit neatly into the rhythmical and alliterative pattern of the verse.

p. 37* (874–900): Stories surrounding Sigemund and Fitela and their family are assumed by the poet to be known to the audience. Other surviving early versions disagree with each other, and it is impossible to know precisely what the poet is alluding to. The main point is to introduce these major heroic figures, including a dragon-slayer, as a means of raising Beowulf to their status.

p. 38* (901–15): Heremod, possibly based on a historical figure, is portrayed as an earlier Danish king who went to the bad and was finally deposed by his subjects.

p. 46* (1066–1159): This account of the Fight at Finnsburg and its aftermath being incomplete implies that the audience is expected to know the story in some detail. A fragment of another Old English poem on the same subject gives further information. The text of this, with parallel translation, is given in *A Choice of Anglo-Saxon Verse*, pp. 16–19. It is not possible to reconstruct the events with complete certainty, but the following is plausible.

A party of Danes under Prince Hnaf is visiting the Frisian king, Finn, who has married Hnaf's sister Hildeburh. It may be that there are Jutes among both the Danish party and Finn's retainers, and it seems that some Jutish dispute causes conflict between the two groups, in the course of which Hnaf and Finn's son are killed. Hengest becomes head of the Danish party. (At this point the account in *Beowulf* begins.) Since it is too late in the season for the Danish party to go home, a truce is agreed, and the Danes are supplied with a hall, apparently shared with the Frisians, who are given strict instructions not to provoke trouble. However some Danes, possibly newly arrived, provoke Hengest in the end to exact revenge, and Finn is killed and Hildeburh taken back to Denmark. (For a full discussion of possible reconstructions see, for example, J. R. R. Tolkien, *Finn and Hengest: The Fragment and the Episode*, ed. Alan Bliss, London, 1982.)

p. 50* (1164), 'still': Old English *gyt*. Typically the poet tells us or implies what is to happen: Hrothulf will fall out with Hrothgar and deprive Hrethric of the succession, causing him to seek asylum at the Geat court.

p. 50† (1172): In the manuscript this is followed by a further suggestion that he should be generous in two lines which seem clearly incomplete, suggesting that a line or more has been lost.

p. 52* (1198–1201): Various accounts are found of Eormenric, an Ostrogothic king of the fourth century, treated in surviving northern European accounts as a tyrant. The poet here alludes to some incident in which Hama apparently removes this famous necklace from Eormenric's hoard and flees, but given the allusive nature of the passage it is impossible to know the details of the event.

p. 52† (1202–4): The first allusion to the disastrous raid into Frisia in which Hygelac was killed.

p. 61* (1392–4): Beowulf uses the masculine pronoun, though Hrothgar has clearly implied just above that it is a female.

p. 73* (1689–93): This refers to the destruction of the Giants by the Flood, Genesis 6:4.

p. 76* (1740): The division of the poem into numbered 'fitts' as in the manuscript generally seems sensible, but this break in mid-sentence is surprising. It could be the result of a scribal slip in placing the number. See too note to p. 88*.

p. 83* (1931), 'Thryth': There are problems in interpreting the text at this point, and even her name is uncertain. Thryth appears as the queen of a historical King Offa of the continental Angles in the late fourth or early fifth century, and is represented as having begun as a cruel princess (or possibly queen) and been tamed after marrying Offa, subsequently acquiring a favourable reputation.

p. 85* (1969), 'young': According to Klaeber's calculations he was about thirty-five when he became king, so scarcely young here; the poet must mean 'vigorous and in command', not 'old' like Hrothgar.

p. 86* (1994–7): This is incompatible with the account given on p. 9, unless one excludes Hygelac from the category of 'wise folk'! There is a similar disparity on pp. 130–1 between what Wiglaf says about having tried to dissuade Beowulf from the dragon fight and what we have previously been told.

p. 88* (2039): The Roman numeral for the 'fitt' has been omitted by the scribe, as has XXXVIIII at p. 120; here it would seem to have been unusually in mid-sentence. There is no sign of a 'fitt' number for XXX in the manuscript, so possibly numbers have gone wrong thereafter.

p. 90* (2097), 'continued to experience life's joys': A striking example of the ironic humour the poet occasionally employs.

p. 101* (2379–96): This recounts part of a series of wars between the Geats and Swedes which are referred to between this point and the end of the poem.

  After the death of the Geatish king Hrethel, the Swedes under Ongentheow attack the country. The new king Hathkin, Hrethel's elder surviving son, mounts a revenge attack on Sweden with some success, including the capture of the Swedish queen. She is rescued in a counter-attack, and the Geats driven into a wood, and Hathkin slain. The remainder are rescued by a force under Hygelac, and Ongentheow is driven back into his fortress, where he is killed defending himself (pp. 105–6 and much more fully at pp. 124–7). His son Ohthere becomes king of the Swedes, followed at his death by Onela, probably 'usurping' from Ohthere's elder son. Later, after the death in battle of Hygelac, when his son Heardred is king of the Geats, the sons of Ohthere, Eanmund and Eadgils, flee the Swedish court and take refuge with the Geats. Onela attacks the Geats, and Eanmund and Heardred are killed, Beowulf becoming king of the Geats. Eadgils attacks Onela, who is killed, and Eadgils becomes king of the Swedes.

p. 101† (2380), 'lake': 'sea' in the original. The poet seems to use various words loosely for stretches of water. See also next note.

p. 102* (2394): It seems that the battle historically took place on the ice of the frozen Lake Väner, though the poem does not say so, and 'frozen' is here added. See Fr. [Friedrich] Klaeber, *Beowulf and the Fight at Finnsburg*, 3rd edition, 1950, p. xliii.

p. 105* (2469), 'chose God's light': This seems to be a euphemism for 'died'.

p. 105† (2472–89): See note to p. 101*, above.

p. 105‡ (2477), 'Hresnaberg': The location of this and other named places is unknown.

p. 106* (2484–9): Eofor's slaying of Ongentheow is described in more detail at p. 126.

p. 106† (2501–2): That is, in the battle when Hygelac was killed.

p. 107* (2517), 'brave': Apparently just a conventional epithet, or perhaps ironic, in view of what is going to happen?

p. 107† (2536): Beowulf here seems to show a particular interest in winning the treasure, as Sigemund did in his dragon fight (see p. 37). Some have argued that this shows a flaw in his character, perhaps even contributing to his failure to survive. It seems more likely that he is simply glad to have won it for the sake of his people and successor. See also pp. 115 and 118.

p. 110* (2611–19): Somewhat surprisingly we learn that Wiglaf's father had fought on the side of Onela against the Swedish princes who had taken refuge at the Geatish court, and he had slain the claimant to the Swedish throne.

p. 117* (2764–6): Another of the rather inept moralising comments which occur from time to time.

p. 118* (2805), 'Hronsness': 'The whale's headland'.

p. 124* (2924–90): A more than usually complete account of a battle; see note to p. 101*.

p. 127* (2994): It is not clear what these units were, or whether of extent or value, but probably the latter.

p. 128* (3004): According to Klaeber and others this is followed by what appears to be an intrusive line, which would need at least to be emended, and is omitted in this translation; but if included it would give: 'After the fall of heroes, brave shield bearers,' referring back apparently to Hygelac's and subsequent Geat defeats.

p. 128† (3014–15): He says fire will consume the treasures; but it seems from p. 134 that they are later buried in the barrow.

p. 130* (3074–5): These two lines seem to be corrupt in the manuscript, and there is no general agreement about their intended meaning.